"In *The Gift of One Day,* Kerry and Chris Shook give us the fresh awareness of what it means to walk with God in one-day wonder, even on our most difficult days."

——Mark Batterson, lead pastor of National Community Church
and *New York Times* best-selling author of *The Circle Maker*

"*The Gift of One Day* will challenge you to never again look at a single day of your life as ordinary. Kerry and Chris will open your eyes to the truth that each day God gives you on this planet is an extraordinary gift to be received, unwrapped, and lived for the glory of the Giver."

——Steven Furtick, founder and lead pastor of Elevation Church
and best-selling author of *(Un)Qualified, Crash the Chatterbox,*
and *Sun Stand Still*

"Out of a poignant story of one brief life comes this book—a source of hope, encouragement, and vision for all who read it. Kerry and Chris Shook have never been the same since their grandchild went to be with the Lord after a single day on earth. Little Jude Samuel Shook changed their perspective forever, and through this inspiring and insightful book, he can change yours as well!"

——Lee Strobel, *New York Times* best-selling author

"Whether you're the strongest believer or the most ardent atheist, a billionaire or totally bankrupt, famous or unknown, you will experience heartache and loss. None of us can avoid trials and tragedy. The question is, What will you do on the worst day of your life? When it comes to unbearable loss, you may never get over it, but with God's power you will get through it! In *The Gift of One Day,* Kerry and Chris Shook come alongside you and share their story of hope. They remind us all that no matter what we're going through, we don't have to go through it alone."

—RICK WARREN, founder and senior pastor of Saddleback Church and best-selling author of *The Purpose-Driven Life*

"When life is hard, every day feels like a mountain to climb. Sometimes the thought of tomorrow is too much to handle. In *The Gift of One Day*, Kerry and Chris Shook share their personal heartache to help you discover the hope, comfort, and strength only God can provide."

—CRAIG GROESCHEL, pastor of Life.Church and *New York Times* best-selling author

"This is a wonderful book about persistent love, tears, mourning, and defiant hope. It is about the raw experience of a family who huddled together through hurt, laughter, and human-angelic encounters and came out of their ordeal with a message of hope from heaven."

—KJELL AXEL JOHANSON, dean emeritus of Woodlands Seminary and author of *God and the Spiritual Tsunami*

"Between the troubles we face and the realization of God's promise that all will be well lies a journey many dread to walk. Although the pain of walking in this deep valley of despair is great, Kerry and Chris Shook allowed God to use their story to teach us how He grows our faith and trust in Him. *The Gift of One Day* shows us a God who cares deeply and who showers us with His wonders a day at a time."

—BISHOP PHILIP KITOTO, general superintendent of the Kenya Assemblies of God

"The love and grace of God pouring out from the pages of this book made an impact on my life. This is an amazing story that teaches us how to grow closer to God even in the most difficult moments of our lives. Thank you, Jude Samuel, for your one day on this planet that is still producing eternal fruit!"

—ABE HUBER, lead pastor of Paz Central Church in São Paulo, Brazil

"Kerry and Chris Shook's faith in God and attitude toward life have inspired me to trust God no matter what happens. I am certain this book will bring you closer to God and give you courage to trust Him in every season of life."

—ANDREAS NIELSEN, lead pastor of Hillsong Sweden

THE
GIFT OF
ONE
DAY

THE
GIFT OF
ONE
DAY

HOW TO FIND HOPE WHEN
LIFE GETS HARD

KERRY & CHRIS
SHOOK

Best-Selling Authors of *One Month to Live*

WATERBROOK

Hardcover ISBN 978-1-60142-726-7
eBook ISBN 978-1-60142-728-1

Cover design by Mark D. Ford

Published in the United States by WaterBrook, an imprint of Random House, a division of Penguin Random House LLC.

WATERBROOK® and its deer colophon are registered trademarks of Penguin Random House LLC.

Library of Congress Cataloging-in-Publication Data
Names: Shook, Kerry, author. | Shook, Chris.
Title: The gift of one day : how to find hope when life gets hard / Kerry Shook and Chris Shook.
Description: Colorado Springs : WaterBrook, 2020. | Includes bibliographical references.
Identifiers: LCCN 2019025435 | ISBN 9781601427267 (hardcover) | ISBN 9781601427281 (ebook)
Subjects: LCSH: Consolation.
Classification: LCC BV4905.3 .S5744 2020 | DDC 248.8/66—dc23
LC record available at https://lccn.loc.gov/2019025435

Printed in the United States of America
2020—First Edition

10 9 8 7 6 5 4 3 2 1

SPECIAL SALES
Most WaterBrook books are available at special quantity discounts when purchased in bulk by corporations, organizations, and special-interest groups. Custom imprinting or excerpting can also be done to fit special needs. For information, please email specialmarketscms@penguinrandomhouse.com.

For Mary Love

Contents

INTRODUCTION
One Day with Jude   1

LESSON 1
When Tomorrow Is Too Much,
Pray _Just for Today, Lord_   17

LESSON 2
You're Dependent on God for Every Breath   31

LESSON 3
If You're Never Mistaken for an Angel,
You're Doing It Wrong   47

LESSON 4
Hard Isn't the Opposite of Good   69

LESSON 5
Everyone Needs a Miracle Book   83

LESSON 6
Share Your Story . . .
Even If You Don't Know How It Ends   95

LESSON 7
When Nothing Makes Sense, Just Obey   107

LESSON 8
Everyone Needs Help, Including You   121

LESSON 9
Fear and Faith Can't Occupy the Same Space   139

LESSON 10
If You're Still Breathing, It's a Good Day   153

LESSON 11
You Don't Have to Pray. You Get to Pray.   167

LESSON 12
It's So Hard Because the Stakes Are So High   179

LESSON 13
There Is a Hidden Gift in Every Hurt   193

LESSON 14
The Number of Your Days Is Unrelated
to the Impact of Your Life   211

ACKNOWLEDGMENTS   221
NOTES   225

One Day with Jude

I, Jude, am a slave to Jesus Christ . . . writing to those loved by God the Father, called and kept safe by Jesus Christ. Relax, everything's going to be all right; rest, everything's coming together; open your hearts, love is on the way!

—JUDE 1:1–2, MSG

He was given the gift of one day. One sunset. One sunrise. Just one rotation of the planet before he left it. Unlike the average American, he wasn't gifted with almost eighty years of life on this earth. He wasn't granted eighty years or eighty days or even eight days. No, he was given the gift of one day.

However, the way Jude Samuel Shook unwrapped the divine gift of his one day gave us, his grandparents, a gift that has changed the way we now live every day. A little boy who lived on this earth for just a handful of hard-fought hours taught us how to live our years.

Ask us what we remember about that day—that particular twenty-four hours from midday on January 7 to midday on January 8, 2017—and we can tell you absolutely everything.

But here's the biggest change of all: ask us what we remember about all the days *since* then, and we can tell you a whole lot more than we could've told you about almost every other day in all the years before it. The intense twenty-four hours we lived on that January day, as well as the things that took place leading up to it, have substantially changed how we approach each new day.

One day turned us upside down. And we've never gotten over it. We never *want* to get over it. One day changed the way we now live *every* day. We pray our story will do the same for you.

Imagine never facing another day just hoping to get through it. Imagine staying alert all day to its vital importance, even with the on-slaught of interruptions and the hypnotic hum of your routine activities. Imagine turning each spare moment into a memory-making encounter for someone you come across. Imagine seeing what's usually unseen in the people and places all around you, things that are all too easy to over-look but that become surprisingly visible when you're viewing them through the eyes of faith and hope, grace and courage.

Imagine each day being different. Imagine the dull becoming excit-ing. Imagine your first thoughts each morning being charged with ener-gizing expectation. Imagine the grocery store cashier going home and telling her husband about this incredible person who said something to her in line today that touched her heart, which hadn't happened in forever.

Imagine one day holding all *that* instead of it being another ordi-nary day.

January 8, 2017, was a really, really, really hard day. We'd hate to live it again. We'd hate to think you'd *ever* need to live it—or anything close to it—just as you'd never wish certain hard days of your own on any-one else.

But something amazing happened. Living through that difficult day refocused our priorities. It altered some habits and attitudes that we'd gradually allowed for our own comfort and protection. It deepened us in places where we preferred living in small-talk safety. It shook up our routines, helping us see our hours as opportunities rather than obligations—as chances to be specific and intentional in our living.

NOTHING SURPRISES GOD

Jude Samuel.

Jude—meaning "praise."

Samuel—meaning "the Lord has heard."

We loved his name from the moment we heard it: "Praise! The Lord has heard."

Jude Samuel Shook is our third grandchild. He's positioned right in the middle of Ben, Joanna, Lincoln, and Mary Love. He is no less or more loved, no less or more treasured, no less or more special than any of our other adorable grandkids. It's just that Jude's story is unique.

Here, let us introduce you to him.

Josh, our middle son, and his wife, Kelli, announced their first pregnancy to us during early summer. And like any parents whose child is expecting, we celebrated their news with giddy excitement for what it meant to their young family, as well as to our larger one.

In no time, of course, all the routine developments and happenings of prenatal life soon commenced—not routine to Josh and Kelli at the time but routine somehow in spite of the always-miraculous process of childbirth. Once Kelli's pregnancy reached the twenty-week mark, having had nothing but textbook-perfect medical visits until that point, the two of them went in for her scheduled checkup with the ob-gyn. Kelli had her first full-body scan to obtain a major set of ultrasound images.

The technology involved in these exams has advanced exponentially through the years. But the thrill of seeing your tiny child on the screen, visibly existing there in the womb, invokes the same level of wonder as in any past generation. Every parent can remember what that moment was like, even if the ultrasounds were too garbled and grainy to ascertain exactly what the technician was showing you. Josh and Kelli were over the moon looking forward to it.

But they were on their knees coming out of it.

Nobody—not us, not them, not even the medical staff who'd been providing high-quality care all along—had seen any signs to indicate what our son and his wife were about to face. The analysis of these twenty-week pictures indicated that Jude was missing his entire left kidney, which was bad, of course, though not fatal in itself.

But missing a kidney wasn't the worst of his problems. The reason this unexpected update was so devastating was that his other kidney—his right kidney—was multicystic and dysplastic. Those are frightening terms that mean his one existing kidney was tumorous (multicystic) as well as enlarged (characterized by dysplasia). It wasn't functioning and could *never* function. Once outside Kelli's body, Jude could not survive with this extreme deficiency.

But not even this was the full extent of concern. The critical condition of his kidneys created other complications that were equally troublesome. Without healthy, functioning kidneys, the amniotic fluid stays below optimal levels. As a result, Jude wasn't quite as comfortable and protected as he should have been. Worse, he was unable to practice breathing in the amniotic fluid. Kelli's body would provide for him while he was in the womb, but his lungs wouldn't be strong enough to sustain him after birth.

As compassionately as possible, the doctor shared the grim news that

Jude would not be able to breathe and would probably be stillborn. Within a matter of moments, Josh and Kelli went from their lives being great to being told their son wouldn't make it.

You can only imagine the heartbreak that followed. Or perhaps you can do more than just imagine it. Maybe you, like us, have experienced the jolt of being plunged from a sunny, expectant outlook to that crushing moment when the room spins, when faces blur. You hear people speaking words that would seem plausible only if they were being said of someone else.

It's all so incredibly disorienting. Unbelievable.

How could this be? Jude? Not well? Not fine? Not progressing according to plan? He'd been developing so effortlessly, it seemed—growing the same way other babies had before and have since. Sure, Josh and Kelli never expected pregnancy to be easy, completely comfortable, or without inconvenience. But they had every reason to expect the next twenty weeks to progress normally, toward the crib and the cadence of the rocking chair, toward the decorated nursery and the dresser filled with tiny newborn clothes.

Now everything was different? Just like that?

Yes, despite how far-fetched it might have seemed when Josh and Kelli went to sleep the night before, we were facing a life-changing tragedy. Oh, how much different tonight's bedtime would be. Tonight there wouldn't be any sleeping at all. For any of us. Our entire family gathered at Josh and Kelli's house. Sobbing. Praying. Begging for a miracle.

We were totally blindsided by the devastating news. We just never saw it coming. But fortunately, there is One who is never blindsided by anything, and His presence was with us that night. Our son Josh was the first to put into words what God was speaking to all our hearts that night when he said, "It's good to know that nothing surprises God. We just found out today, but God has known Jude's condition all along. He's not surprised by this, and He's the one writing Jude's story. So we'll trust Him."

Maybe you've been blindsided by devastating events in your life. Perhaps you've had the kind of gut-wrenching, knocked-to-your-knees moment when your world came crashing down all around you.

You go into work one morning and come home without a job at the end of the day. You begin planning a vacation but receive a doctor's report that leaves you wondering whether you'll still be here that far into the future. You start the day full of hope, but before the end of the day, you've discovered your spouse has been unfaithful and you're reeling from the betrayal.

Remember, no matter what has unexpectedly smashed into your life, God wasn't surprised by it. God didn't cause it, but He wasn't blindsided by it. He was grieving for you before you even knew about it. Nothing surprises God, and He's the one writing your story. And guess what? He's not finished writing!

It gave us so much comfort to know that even though we were numb from the shocking news, God wasn't and He would keep guiding us along the way. We could trust Him with the unknown.

A DIFFERENT KIND OF MIRACLE

Unable to sleep the night after the diagnosis, our oldest son, Ryan, began digging around on the internet for everything related to these multi-syllable medical terms we weren't sure we'd ever heard—and certainly not in connection with anyone in our family. Somewhere in the course of his search, he hit upon something—an article containing information about an experimental program conducted at the Cincinnati Children's

Hospital, which reported having limited success treating unborn children who suffered from the same or similar conditions as Jude.

Okay, well . . . what should we do? Should we call them? I mean, if there's a one-in-a-thousand—even a one-in-a-*million*—chance you can save your child or grandchild's life, you take it, right? Isn't that better than just accepting his approaching death as inevitable?

So within seventy-two hours of receiving Jude's diagnosis, Josh and Kelli were on a plane headed for Cincinnati, Ohio, where they would spend the next two months, along with various members of our family who visited or stayed with them. During that time they meticulously followed the protocols the team of doctors was using—efforts that held out a glimmer of hope that our little Jude could fight through his multitude of dreadfully critical setbacks and come out on the other side a champion.

That's what we prayed for. Incessantly. Passionately.

Yes, we knew the odds were stacked solidly against him. The doctors and nurses, who were absolutely wonderful, pulled no punches in describing just how tough this road would be, even in the best case. No one gave any of us what you'd call an optimistic prognosis, except to tell us that it had been done before, that it was not impossible. Success rates only in the single percentage points maybe, and yet . . . a pulse, a prayer.

So with only this spiderweb fragment of hope to hold on to, we prayed for a miracle, knowing all the time that we were praying huge— praying way bigger than we'd probably ever prayed for anything.

Yet in the end, things didn't happen how we wanted.

Which hasn't stopped hurting, even now.

The book you're about to read isn't the story we wish it were; it is not the story of Jude's heroic, miraculous victory despite enormous medical obstacles. We miss him every day and ache to see our son and his wife endure the pain. We'll share a lot more with you about what happened, as well as the takeaways we've gleaned from the narrow parameters of Jude's life—his one day of life. We are *still* learning from these experiences, so much so that we wanted to bring you along as we unpack how all of us can spend the rest of our days on things that really matter.

But here's the miracle: Jude's story is a good one. It's not the one we would have written, but despite all the hard and hurt, God has made it good. God has made it right.

EVERYTHING IS GOING TO BE ALL RIGHT

Not long after Jude went home to be with the Lord, our daughter, Megan, sent a group text to everyone in our family. She quoted a couple of verses from the beginning of the tiny New Testament letter ascribed to Jude, the half brother of Jesus.

Perhaps because of the name they share, we'd each found ourselves turning to that book often, searching for meaning and comfort. With just twenty-five verses, it barely occupies a full page. When we received Megan's message, the book of Jude wasn't on our minds at all, but as soon as her text came through, it was as though *our* Jude were speaking to us directly from heaven. These were among the most encouraging words of our lives spoken at the single most discouraging time: "I, Jude, am a slave to Jesus Christ . . . writing to those loved by God the Father, called and kept safe by Jesus Christ. Relax, everything's going to be all right; rest, everything's coming together; open your hearts, love is on the way!" (1:1–2, MSG).

Wow.

Every day after Jude's negative prognosis had been a battle. We'd been laser focused on doing whatever it took to get both Jude and Kelli into the best possible shape, beseeching the Lord to intervene. It was one high-intensity day after another, after another. And then—

It just stopped. In a heartbeat. And it left us feeling as if we were still out on that racetrack, bursts of adrenaline coursing through our veins, yet the finish line had suddenly disappeared.

But the truth of those two verses just reached out and grabbed us and pulled us close. The Lord, as He often does, had come and found us in our emptiness, in our sadness. And through words He'd written long centuries before, He said to us, "Relax . . . rest . . . open your hearts."

"Everything's going to be all right."

Not "all right" as in "okay." But all right.

When everything in our world felt and looked all wrong, God was reminding us through Jude that everything would be all right.

A lot of things are not all right in our broken, decaying world.

But someday.

One day.

All that is wrong will be made all right.

For many of us, our instinctive reaction is "Things turn out all right? No—things *don't* turn out all right." Maybe they don't necessarily get worse—you might be thinking, *How could they* be *much worse?*—but except for time dulling the edges of the pain, maybe your life experience hasn't shown you this truth.

Sometimes the only thing harder than going through the suffering itself is trying to piece together a logical explanation for it. The hardship is real. And the answers, the dots, the clues that might yield some measure of comprehension or reveal purpose in what you're going through can feel like guesses and rationalizations at best. It doesn't matter whom you ask or how hard you try to think and pray about it, the whys just keep gnawing away.

Let us be clear: We're not trying to explain all suffering. Nor are we naively hinting that you will witness a complete resolution of your ordeal within the limited space of your lifetime and that if you don't, you're lacking in some spiritual area or harboring a pessimistic, sorry-for-yourself attitude.

Truth is, it's not all right that you've experienced intense loss or are aching with grief. It's not all right that Jude's not here. It's not all right that Josh and Kelli have been forced to endure the things they have. It's not all right when we gather as an extended family and Jude is absent. It's not all right. It's messed up. It is *not* all right.

That Jude was given only one day on this earth feels all wrong, but we know that one day God will make it all right and we will be with Jude every day for eternity.

If we're honest, this is easier to believe at certain times than at others. Yet already, in small ways and occasionally really big ways, God keeps giving us evidence that whispers to our grieving hearts, *It's going to be all right.*

NOT ONE DAY LESS

Since baby Jude went to live there, God has given us a one-day insight into heaven and eternity that we had never quite grasped.

During those frantic few hours when Josh and Kelli were working hard to secure a spot in the Cincinnati program, Josh made a statement that settled all our hearts, one that speaks to the confidence a relationship with God brings within tangible reach of all His children. Obviously, Josh and Kelli wanted as much time with Jude as possible, to make the most of every moment with him. Obviously, they wanted to do whatever they could do to make him comfortable, to give him room to grow and develop without restriction. "But no matter what happens," Josh said, "whether he lives a day or a hundred years, we'll still have no fewer days to spend with him in heaven."

That's what eternity does for us.

Eternity brings peace. Eternity brings hope. Eternity weighs in when life outweighs us.

Our future may indeed be as full as the Bible says, but it still feels empty right now. God understands we do not possess the natural capacity to trust in eternity whenever He chooses not to give us what we want on this earth. But the future He's promised us is *secure*. The future we struggle to bank on is *real*.

Jude *is* with the Lord. We *will* see him again. And the time we'll have with him, despite how briefly we got to be with him here, will not be diminished even one day because of it.

The apostle Paul instructed us to "encourage one another with these words" (1 Thessalonians 4:18), these biblical truths that affirm the sure coming of eternity, because no loss, not even the loss of death, is "able to separate us from the love of God" (Romans 8:39). God, who could have allowed this sin-cursed, death-confined planet to be the last word on all our suffering, has instead given us the hope of eternity.

And if we'll look for it, we can actually see hope for eternity wherever we are today.

LIFE LESSONS

If this experience with Jude has taught us anything, it's that we're still learning. We've got a long way to go. We are still figuring out how to internalize and articulate all these life lessons we've been given and apply them to our lives.

But we'll tell you this: we are changing in specific, practical ways.

And maybe you'd like to change with us.

Knowing that one day everything will be all right is comforting, but we found ourselves asking, *How am I going to make it through this day?*

That's the focus of this book. The lessons God taught us through Jude have been our lifeline for making it through one day at a time, one breath at a time—unwrapping each day as a sacred gift from God by opening our hearts to receive the love He brings every day.

We still don't understand why God chose to end Jude's life on earth so soon. We miss him. We want him in our arms. But what comforts us is this: during the one day God set aside for him to be here with us before choosing to call him home, Jude obeyed his Father's will. The Lord asked only that he be Jude Samuel. And because he did his best to fill up those lungs with all the breath his little body could muster, God worked through that thin wisp of air to bless us with a lasting prize from that day.

This realization made us wonder: On how many of our "one days" have we made even a breath of difference in the lives of others? We think of days we've wasted, when we've been selfish or just wandered through aimlessly.

It's taken a little boy doing everything he was meant to do during his one day on earth to help us see the truth that God can take one day, totally surrendered to Him, and do something through it that lasts for eternity.

The day before we headed to Cincinnati, loaded down with all our fears, hopes, and confusion, we packed a blank journal that we called the Miracle Book. We decided to start writing down all the miracles we saw God doing through our journey into the unknown, and we're so glad we did. After Jude went to heaven, we got the book out, read through it, and realized it was filled with life-altering lessons God had taught us along the way.

The Miracle Book is now one of our most prized possessions, and we want to share it with you. The fourteen lessons outlined in this book have changed the way we approach each and every day God gives us.

No matter where you find yourself right now—whether you have serious hurts that you want to learn how to walk through with your shoulders straight, you're stuck in a rut and eager to escape it, or you simply want to stop letting your days slip by without leaving a significant mark—we welcome you on this journey. Whatever your reason, we believe God wants to teach you something through the one-day life of one tiny, helpless, fragile boy; his courageous parents; and the people we met on this journey.

It's our prayer that these lessons from Jude will open your heart and help you learn how to boldly unwrap the gift of one day.

When Tomorrow Is Too Much, Pray *Just for Today, Lord*

God said, "Let there be light," and there was light. God saw that the light was good, and he separated the light from the darkness. God called the light "day," and the darkness he called "night." And there was evening, and there was morning—the first day.

—Genesis 1:3–5

Millions long for immortality who don't know what to do with themselves on a rainy Sunday afternoon.

—Susan Ertz

sn't that passage from Genesis 1 beautiful? Both in its power and in its simplicity? Darkness and light. Evening and morning. These were the basic elements of "the first day."

They are also the basic elements of *every* day. Of *this* day: today.

A day was one of the first things God made. Before He made starfish and eagles and mountains and people, He created a day. Before even making the sun and the moon, He chose to frame the manner in which He wanted us to experience life. Right from the start, our time here on earth was to be measured in days with an ending and a beginning. Evening and morning.

This has continued and will continue for as long as the earth exists. Life is a stitching together of days. We encounter life—and we encounter God—one day at a time.

Just sit with that idea for a moment. Ponder the reality of what this pattern suggests, what a gift it really is. The structure of what we know as a day is not merely a random measurement of time. God made *this* day *this* way for a reason. He makes *all* our days this way. For a reason.

I mean, think of all the other ways He could have made them.

What if the sun could never be counted on to come up at all? What if you just never knew? It might rise in ten minutes; it might not rise for ten years. Can you imagine? How different life would be—how much scarier and more disorienting—if each morning and evening didn't arrive as reliably as clockwork.

Every day is designed by God with precision, with purpose, with a plan, with importance.

Every day is a new treasure.

But we don't see days that way, do we? When we look at an average day, we see something else. Perhaps we see a canvas that's nowhere near big enough to hold all the things we need to cram into it before tomorrow comes. Or we see a dull, monotonous repeat of the same old tasks and routines. Or we see a basketful of worries and questions and challenges we don't want to face. Or because of regrets and the consequences of our actions, we can't really see much promise in today, having become so controlled by the past.

We don't typically see the treasure in each day. We don't recognize it as a gift. We don't start out often enough asking ourselves, *What am I going to do with this day?*

But what if we did?

What if we did?

How much different would our days become?

JUST FOR TODAY

We arrived in Cincinnati early in November, riding a wave of fresh unknowns. Swinging our feet to the floor the next morning, all we knew
was that we'd followed the trail of hope to this town, to these people. But
what it meant for that day exactly—and for however many more days
might follow—we really had no way of gauging. All we knew to do was
to get up, start walking, and find out.

We understood the gist of the process in broad terms. After a slew of
initial tests, scans, and consultations, Kelli would undergo a surgical procedure. The doctors would implant an amnioport in her abdomen that
would enable her to receive amniotic fluid infusions directly into her
uterus. The operation involved a measure of risk, but if it was completed
according to plan, doctors could supply enough amniotic fluid around
Jude to decrease any discomfort he was experiencing, encouraging his
growth and allowing him to "practice breathe" to strengthen his lungs.
Nothing, of course, could immediately correct the problems he had with
his kidney. But the more these infusions could prolong Kelli's pregnancy
(her due date was still nearly twenty weeks out), the greater the chance of
success.

Success in this case meant that if Kelli was able to deliver Jude and if
the medical team was able to stabilize his little body after birth—which
the odds were stacked against—he'd immediately be put on dialysis. (Dialysis, you probably know, is a procedure that filters the blood, perform-
ing various tasks that normal kidneys naturally do.) Then, under close
monitoring, if he continued to make it past a number of milestones that
indicated his body was strengthening the way it should, the ultimate goal
was that by the time Jude was around two years old, Josh would donate

one of his kidneys to his son. And if all went well with *that,* Jude would be one of the few poster children for this experimental procedure.

That was the long-shot scenario we locked on to with every prayer, with every dream. And we kept walking toward it with each new day that dawned.

Morning and evening.

Morning and evening.

That's how we learned to live.

Each day took on its own meaning and sense of progress. The cliché you hear about living life one day at a time had never seemed so unavoidable, so absolutely necessary. The line we prayed more often than any other, and with more intensity than ever, was this: *Just for today, Lord . . .*

- *Just for today, Lord, give us the strength to endure whatever hard things we have to face, whether we think we can keep going or not.*
- *Just for today, Lord, provide us with the wisdom to know what to do, which questions to ask, and how to prioritize all the things we need to take care of.*
- *Just for today, Lord, help us respond kindly to people who may frustrate or irritate us.*
- *Just for today, Lord, help us not to give up. Not us, not Kelli, not Josh, and not Jude.*
- *Just for today, Lord, meet the needs You know we have.*
- *Just for today, Lord, hold us close.*

Asking Him for tomorrow seemed like asking too much. The weight of the day we were in was all we could focus on. Have you ever been there? Maybe you're there now. Jesus said, "Do not worry about tomorrow, for tomorrow will worry about itself" (Matthew 6:34). Similarly, dwelling on the challenges of yesterday felt like borrowing trouble we couldn't afford—not if we expected to make it to the end of the day. The only way we could deal with the long road ahead of us was to break it down into manageable pieces. *Just for today, Lord.*

Just for today.

Now that our true condition was exposed, these two verses became the bookends of our days:

> Every morning
>> I lay out the pieces of my life
>> on your altar
>> and watch for fire to descend. (Psalm 5:3, MSG)

> At day's end I'm ready for sound sleep,
> For you, GOD, have put my life back together. (4:8, MSG)

We began each morning with a laser-like focus: *Lord, please get us through this day.* Our awareness of our absolute inability to manage even the smallest detail of Jude's life made us rely on God for every hour, every breath. And since we were already trusting Him with the most important thing, it was easy to trust Him with everything else.

It was during this time of intense reliance on God that we realized we were finally seeing our true condition. We'd *always* needed God for absolutely everything! *All* the days of our lives so far had been stuffed with His provision, but we'd allowed ourselves to somehow take credit. Sure, we admitted God helped us—but only in a supporting role. We were a team with God. As if our Creator needed us to help Him!

There's actually a quite profound biblical precedent for living this way. Think of what you remember about the words of Jesus's model prayer—what's come to be known as the Lord's Prayer. It begins (say it with us), "Our Father which art in heaven, hallowed be thy name. Thy kingdom come, thy will be done in earth, as it is in heaven" (Matthew 6:9–10, KJV). Then comes the line that speaks so directly, yet so simply, about what we can expect from God and how He wants us to look to Him: "Give us this day our daily bread" (verse 11, KJV).

Only seven words. And two of them tell us about living in the moment with Him: "Give us *this* day our *daily* bread."

We should've realized the importance of this basic truth sooner in life. The first thing we're taught to pray, after we've praised our heavenly Father and aligned ourselves in faith under His will and purpose, is to ask Him specifically and expectantly for "daily bread." But notice it's perfectly in line with how God has created us to live from the beginning. We ask Him for this day's bread. We lift to Him this day's need. We walk with Him through this day's minutes and hours. We keep ourselves tucked inside this day's grace and provision.

How are you responding to this idea? Maybe it doesn't feel as groundbreaking to you as it became for us as we watched our son and daughter-in-law work so hard each day at trusting and believing and enduring and staying strong. And maybe it shouldn't be. Living with a daily-bread mentality should probably be common enough and shouldn't strike us as being in such stark contrast to our standard way of thinking and operating.

But, boy, doesn't it feel different? Different from our usual?

Here you are—today—living your life. You're surely dealing with a number of things that could create anxiety. You have certain decisions to make. Maybe there's a misunderstanding you need to untangle. You're most likely thinking of several matters lingering somewhere in the back of your mind, whether they are coming up in a week or in a month. Perhaps they're things you've been putting off, but you know you'll eventually need to stop delaying and deal with them. All this stuff, just swirling around in your head.

But what if instead of dwelling on this huge landscape of next weeks and last years and childhood memories and dreams for six months from now, you yanked the curtains in hard from both sides so the new image through your viewfinder is only what is pertinent to today? Nothing you've just obscured really matters at present, except how it influences today. Except what it means for today. *Just for today, Lord.* What if you could box this stuff of life down—the full weight of everything you've been carrying—to only what would fit inside today? Would that change anything for you?

Whenever we allow our minds to be consumed by the plans we're making for later—whenever we refuse to rein in our emotions and fears of what *might* happen—we functionally stop living in today. Our bodies and brains are here, but our souls are mostly somewhere else. We've stopped occupying this daily space where God created us to live. And therefore, His daily bread that He's promised us doesn't feel like enough. We demand that He show us *all* the meals, or we assume He's fine with watching us go hungry.

God created us as daily creatures. He has assured us He will provide an abundance of daily bread. Our role is to discipline our attention and stay focused on only those things we're colliding with today. To stay in our place at the table. Where there is always enough bread.

Just for today, Lord.

A Day's Difference

Before this issue emerged with Josh, Kelli, and Jude, our lives were pretty busy, just as yours is. Unbearably busy, it often seemed. We had dealt with our fair share of difficulties, as well as tending to other people's hurts and needs in the everyday outflow of our ministry—so we thought we knew what stress was like.

But . . . no.

We didn't know.

Spending time around a children's hospital will reconfigure your perspective on that.

We didn't have to watch our grandchild endure pain each day as we noted his wearied facial expression or as his tears wet our collars after a difficult procedure. Jude was there, of course, and was constantly on our minds, but at the same time, he didn't need to be visited, consoled, and encouraged from our depleted resources. So while we definitely were struggling, we didn't face a lot of the situations we saw and heard about from other folks in the hospital.

What we learned and witnessed during that time was both inspiring and heartbreaking. Such incredible people going through such unending crises.

The first thing you notice about families enduring long-term stays at a children's hospital is the constancy of it. Having a sick child just consumes your life. Twenty-four hours a day, seven days a week. With never a break. That would be hard enough all by itself, separate from everything else, but it's *not* isolated from everything else. Life goes on. The bills still need to be paid; the house still needs attention. And what's more—this is the part we'd somehow never realized to such an extent before—many parents have *other* children they need to make arrangements for, even as their time is being understandably monopolized by caring for their child in the hospital. And they may be far from home, as we were, having to juggle everything from a distance, with one or the other parent often traveling back and forth. You can see the stress in their eyes. You can sense its impact on their marriages. You know for sure there is financial stress, from both the staggering medical bills and the loss of income from the parent who's stationed there away from work.

When we talk about staying positioned inside each day, we're not just waxing philosophical. We're not trying to oversimplify the putting together of misshapen parts that can be so incredibly sharp and heavy and impossible to assemble. Not only have we dealt with this reality ourselves, but we've also seen it in others. We've heard some of their war stories, shared with us in conversation.

We're certainly not suggesting your problems would all go into nice, neat little piles if you'd just learn to think a bit differently about everything. Viewing your life more in terms of its daily needs and God's daily provision will never completely smooth out those rough patches that are sure to occur. We don't want to minimize *anything* about what you're going through or downplay how truly overwhelming it can be.

All we're saying is that tomorrow is too big for us. We weren't made for it. We were made for *today*. We were made to consume *daily* bread.

And when we do this, He is able to make it more than enough . . . even on those days that seem like way, way, way too much.

Without God's moment-to-moment sustenance, we knew we'd go under. It came as a complete surprise that this realization didn't leave us feeling abandoned. In fact, we felt His protection most acutely in the hard times, just as the psalmist described:

> I was pushed back and about to fall,
>   but the LORD helped me.
> The LORD is my strength and my defense;
>   he has become my salvation. (118:13–14)

God had been rescuing us every day of our lives, and He wasn't about to stop when things got difficult. For the first time in our lives, we realized that God was truly our everyday salvation! Scripture is clear: "Indeed, the 'right time' is now. Today is the day of salvation" (2 Corinthians 6:2, NLT).

God's salvation is found in today. We'll never find His provision for today by looking for it in tomorrow. That means when tomorrow overwhelms you, all you need is God's saving strength for today. *Just for today, Lord.*

Living the Lesson

When Tomorrow Is Too Much, Pray *Just for Today, Lord*

What are some of the stresses, problems, or distractions that keep you from seeing each day as a gift?

What do you think would change in your life if you began to see each day as a gift from God?

Do you have a deep hurt, hardship, or worry that makes tomorrow feel overwhelming? Read Matthew 6:9–11 and Psalm 118:13–14. How can you begin to live with a daily-bread mentality?

Write your own *Just for today, Lord* prayer in the space below. Today, when you start to feel overwhelmed by tomorrow, pray your *Just for today, Lord* prayer.

Grab a blank notebook or start a new note on your phone or computer to begin your own miracle book. Ask God to open your eyes to see the treasures, big and small, that He's providing, and get in the habit of recording them in your miracle book before the sun goes down.

You're Dependent on God for Every Breath

Then the Lord God formed a man from the dust of the ground and breathed into his nostrils the breath of life, and the man became a living being.

—Genesis 2:7

It's a dangerous business . . . going out of your door.

—J. R. R. Tolkien

Life is all about breathing. If you can't breathe, you can't live. Of course, we all know that. We just don't think much about breathing because our brain stems keep us inhaling and exhaling whether it crosses our minds or not. During those weeks in Cincinnati, Jude made us stop and think a lot about the importance of breathing. So many of our thoughts, prayers, and conversations revolved around Jude being able to breathe when he was born.

As soon as we arrived in Cincinnati, Kelli started receiving injections of amniotic fluid in hope of strengthening Jude's lungs enough that he would be able to breathe outside the womb when the time came. In addition to causing us to think about the necessity of breathing, Jude made us stop and realize how much we depended on God for every breath.

We'd never noticed this truth so clearly on days when we were at home in Houston, where we could fool ourselves into thinking we didn't always need Him. For *some* things, yes, but not for *most* things. We had friends and family to help with most things. And for a lot of things, we didn't need anybody else at all because we know our way around. We know which aisle at Kroger carries the bread and the salad dressing. We know whom to call if the car battery goes dead. We know when church starts and exactly how to get there. We know the teller at the bank, the personnel at the post office, and the staff at the dentist's office, and they all know us. At home we have our routine schedule, including garbage pickup and weekly errands. We've got it all covered. *Thanks for the offer, Lord, but we're good. We've got it.*

We pride ourselves on being able to land in any country and make our way around. God apparently knew that if we were ever going to understand the depth of our dependence on Him, He would need to take us to an entirely different part of the country for an extended period of time so He could show us something in *that* part of the world that is true in *every* part of the world. Even in *our* little corner of the world. Even when we're surrounded by all the stuff that camouflages how deeply and desperately we need Him.

Maybe you, like us, know this is something you haven't been recognizing . . . at least not as clearly as you should.

We. *Need*. Him.

We need Him every day for every breath.

There were so many moments while we were away when this realization just struck us like an open palm to the forehead. *Oh wow, Lord, we really can't go on without You. We need You for everything. What in the world has been distracting us so much that we haven't noticed this before? We cannot last a minute without leaning on You. We are lost without You.*

We felt overwhelmed at times by waves of doubt or dread, thinking if God didn't come through with some good news for us today—if something encouraging didn't happen in the next ten or twenty minutes—we might not be able to hold it all together. He was our only chance, our only hope. There was no doubt about it. None of our neighbors or church friends were going to show up with what we needed. They wouldn't just be stopping by on their way somewhere to see whether they could help us or cheer us up. We realized, *Wow, oh wow, this is how You want us to live* every day, *not looking* anywhere *but to You for our help and relief.*

We were often wrung out with exhaustion, running on near-zero reserves and energy. We wondered how we were going to make it—and we weren't even the patient! Poor Kelli was the one dealing with the worst of the physical drawdown, facing one procedure after another. You could tell how taxing each day was becoming on her body. But together we realized, *Wow—every breath really* does *come from You, God. If not for You, we have* no *provision.*

We'd reach the end of the day wishing for a long, hot shower; wishing we could curl up underneath the covers in our own bed at home; wishing for something as simple yet unattainable as padding around the kitchen in our pj's to grab a favorite snack from the fridge or pantry. We needed and wanted so much that we couldn't have. Yet we'd think, *Yeah, but—wow—what we needed more than anything today was Your comfort, Lord, and You provided it. You did it. We wouldn't have made it without You. Wow, God! Here we are. You did it again!*

We don't know the last time you may have felt that way. And to be honest, before our time in Cincinnati, we don't know whether we could tell you the last time *we'd* felt it.

But we can tell you this: whether we feel it or recognize it or want to believe it, *that's how it really is*! All the time. We are utterly dependent on the Lord for each sweep of the second hand. Our true condition in life is this: you and I cannot get to the next hour, let alone the next day or next year, unless God gets us there.

It's About Time

We've been reading Henri Nouwen lately. He was a Dutch priest and the author of dozens of books, and his meditations are rich with insights on Christian spirituality. Recently we were struck by one of his writings in which he was comparing two words in the Greek language that relate to time.

Chronos is time's more linear aspect, which is how we generally perceive time. Even just seeing the word, you probably make immediate connections to English words such as *chronology, chronological,* and *chronicle. Chronos* describes the *tick-tick-tick* of the clock, as well as time measured across a timeline.[1] It's our internal gauge of how long it takes to complete a certain task, as well as the pressure involved in assembling our calendars—in assembling our lives—so that everything somehow squeezes into our days without squeezing us to death in the process.

We realize that we can't control chronos time. It keeps progressing at the same steady, pounding, *chronological* cadence—unrelenting, undeterred. But we take what time gives us, and we do our best to make it work for us. To maximize it if we can. We determine how *we're* going to arrange it so that it looks like *we* want it to look. We harness it for our personal schedules, thereby exerting a sense of ownership over our lives. Self-management. Self-sufficiency. Independence.

But the ancient Greeks realized time wasn't limited to this scalable, straightforward concept. That's why they coined another word—

kairos—that describes how time contains opportunity.[2] Not only is time a fill-in-the-blank grid of meetings and appointments, but it is also an ongoing opportunity to change. It is the space in which we can recognize larger elements at work in our day, beyond our ten o'clock haircut and lunch with a friend. Kairos enables us to peer inside all the closed, shaded blocks on our daily agendas and instead see openings for deepening our connection with other people, growing our ability to serve and learn and develop, and increasing our understanding of what's *real*—more real than another sales call with a prospective client or the car pool line at school.

Among other things, a kairos perspective helps us see each moment as being under the control, provision, power, grace, kindness, and tender mercy of God. Henri Nouwen put it this way: "Looked upon from below, it's *chronos;* I have to survive, and I have to fight my way through it. Looked at from above, it is *kairos;* it's the opportunity to change your heart in everything you do."[3]

We had been looking at our time and our individual days "from below." We'd accustomed ourselves to seeing them as manageable properties, as things we could handle. Even with the stuff we couldn't quite handle, we knew we could figure out a way. We'd just need to multiply ourselves somehow, muscle through it. Either that or just give up and concede defeat. One or the other.

But those aren't the only options left to a child of God. We can choose to look at our days "from above." We still approach them with our best effort, yes, but we do so without bearing the full burden of responsibility for every outcome, for making the day go exactly the way everybody is expecting us to make it go. Best of all, we can live each day with a settled faith that doesn't pretend we can ultimately do anything more than fall on our faces before Him and trust Him to know precisely what we need, far better than we know it, and then to give it in whatever measure He knows is enough for us.

What an opportunity He gives us every day—the kairos to depend on Him in the midst of our chronos.

FROM *WHY, LORD?* TO *WHAT, LORD?*

Many times when we find ourselves in those places where our total dependence on God becomes more exposed and acute, we start asking Him questions. And the first, most natural question we ask is "Why?" *Why, Lord? Why is this happening? Why us? Why me?*

Certainly, we asked some of those questions ourselves. We kept pleading with Him. We couldn't understand. We did not want to be in such a touch-and-go situation with our grandson, and we obviously wanted a positive outcome. Why did it need to be this way? This was supposed to be a happy and exciting time, not painful and hard.

But once God had peeled us far enough away from our home and our normal routine and had shown us just how faithfully and completely He had our backs, we came to the realization that "Why?" is not really the right question. Because once you've trusted Him with everything, you can trust Him with "Why?" as well. You don't need Him to answer that question for you anymore. The things you do next are not dependent on understanding the reason for the situation you are in.

The better questions, really, are "What?" and "How?" *What does obedience look like today, Lord? How does my utter dependence on You change how I live these next twenty-four hours?* Suddenly your day transforms from chronos to kairos. To an acceptance of reality. You intentionally ground yourself in the fact that He is taking care of *all* of it. He is doing *everything*. He will *never* lose sight of you or fail to provide what you need. He will be your *only* source and supply, even if He conscripts other people, even strangers, to be the vehicle. Your only job is to lean on Him and let Him care for you and give Him the opportunity to demonstrate through your life the amazing things He can do.

This reminds us of something God conveyed to Paul—a statement that sounds crazy until God puts you in circumstances where you can see for yourself the stark limitations of your own resources. "My grace is sufficient for you," God promised him, "for my power is made perfect in weakness" (2 Corinthians 12:9). From this Paul concluded, "Therefore I will boast all the more gladly about my weaknesses, so that Christ's power may rest on me. That is why, for Christ's sake, I delight in weaknesses, in insults, in hardships, in persecutions, in difficulties. For when I am weak, then I am strong" (verses 9–10).

Reality will give you that kind of perspective on things. Reality says weakness is what we want. Reality says dependence is how we experience completeness. Reality says we don't need excitement or fun or comfort or safety—we just need Jesus. Because if we have Him, He'll make us strong.

That's the place you want to live every day. It may not *feel* like home, but it's actually where you've been all along.

So here we are, back in Houston now. Where we like it. We've got our schedule for the day laid out in front of us—various interactions, generally with people we already know, at places we need no directions to find. Things are mostly back to normal.

But our goal is to live today like we're in Cincinnati. Back when we were making the choice, moment by moment, to put our full confidence in the Lord, knowing with the rawest certainty that we had nowhere else to turn. Back when every morning we would start out praying with focused intensity, doubling down on the promises of God, realizing our own strength and resolve promised us nothing. And back when at the end of each day, we'd look around and say, "He did it again, guys. He got us through. He never stops doing it."

Because we never stop needing Him.

Even when we think we've got it ourselves.

A BEAUTIFUL CRY

We never felt the truth of our dependence on God more than the day Kelli went into labor. For weeks we had been preparing for this day, but we knew it was all in God's hands.

The delivery room at Good Samaritan Hospital was jam-packed with medical personnel and staffed with at least ten people from the neonatal intensive care unit (NICU), along with all their gear and equipment. Each of us knew our place. The hospital staff and doctors, who were so great to us the whole time, made sure it was all perfectly choreographed. As soon as Jude was born, they were to intubate him and whisk him off to the NICU. Josh and Chris would follow them while Kelli's mom and other team members wheeled Kelli into surgery to remove her port.

Everything needed to happen with precision. Unlike a more routine birth, where the baby's entry into the open air is greeted with deep sighs of relief and hearty congratulations, Jude's delivery set off a wave of fast-moving action, shouted commands, and clipped numerical responses. Kelli and Josh were working hard as a team to bring their long-awaited boy into the world.

We'd been told to expect that Jude would struggle right from the outset. Normal processes (such as his lung function, for instance) might not be working at all. But finally *there he was*—Jude!—so precious, even if so tiny and underweight. After all those weeks of hard work, prayer, and interminable waiting, we got a quick look at that pink skin, at that trembling body, at those moving arms and legs. It was beyond thrilling. It was love at first sight!

And then . . . a sound.

He cried.

Jude *cried*! It lasted no more than a few seconds. But it was glorious, a holy shout they said we almost certainly wouldn't hear—not only because of the weakness of his lungs but also because of how quickly they'd have him hooked up to a device to assist with his breathing. Yet in the sliver of time before they hooked him up to that snaking network of tubes and machines, Jude announced his presence to the world.

Oh, to see his face. *And* to hear his voice!

It was one of the most beautiful sounds ever heard. Newborn cries can be so shrill and grating. But do you know how we cherish the treasure of that tiny interrupted cry? Can you imagine what it's like for Josh and Kelli now to be able to close their eyes, return to that moment, and draw their son's cry out of the folds of their memories, like the fading scent of perfume on a handwritten letter?

It was like the aroma rising from a loaf of fresh bread. It was the Father's sweet answer to our *Just for today* prayer on that day—giving us the lifelong treasure of Jude's cry to join the chorus of our own cries in the days that followed so soon, so sadly. The Lord knew what we needed. That cry was His gift. He gave Jude a voice that day, and it is still warming our hearts.

When you cry out to your heavenly Father, He hears your cry and holds it like a priceless treasure. Whether it's a cry of deep anguish, anger, or desperation, God always hears a beautiful sound coming from His child that He loves so much.

The psalmist tells us,

> Trust in him at all times, you people;
>> pour out your hearts to him,
>> for God is our refuge. (62:8)

God wants us to pour out our hearts to Him, even if we cry out in frustration, anger, and confusion. Our cries to God reveal how much we need Him. Just as the cries of newborns reveal how dependent they are on others to take care of their every need, our cries to God confess our complete dependence on Him. When we use our breath to cry out to God, we are just admitting the reality of our condition—we need God for our next breath.

LET EVERYTHING THAT HAS BREATH

When we cry out to God in our desperation, He begins to turn our cries to praise as we see how much we can trust Him with our next breath. Every night in Cincinnati as Josh and Kelli were waiting for Jude to be born, Josh would get out his guitar, and he and Kelli would sing praise songs. The chorus of one of the songs they sang every night says,

> It's Your breath in our lungs
> So we pour out our praise to You only.[4]

It is God who puts breath in our lungs, and He wants us to use each breath to bring honor and glory to Him. We need God for every breath, and we have God for every breath. So just for today, breathe out God's praise. Just for today, breathe in God's grace and breathe out His graciousness on everyone you meet. Just for this moment, breathe in God's strength and breathe out gratitude to Him for holding you together when everything feels like it's falling apart. Just breathe. Just breathe. It's really all about breathing.

Living the Lesson

You're Dependent on God for Every Breath

Is there a situation in your life that you've been trying to fix or control that has proved to be unfixable or uncontrollable?

Read 2 Corinthians 12:9–10. Your greatest weakness or problem is God's greatest opportunity to demonstrate His strength in your life. How is your situation helping you learn to depend on God's strength rather than your own?

When we feel angry, hurt, or confused, it's important to express our *Why, Lord?* questions to God. Write down some of your questions regarding your current situation. Don't hold back. Remember, God always hears your cries because you are His child and He loves you!

Why, Lord? questions help us grieve our hurts, but only *What, Lord?* questions help us move forward in healing. List some *What, Lord?* questions that could change your perspective today.

Write a prayer to the Lord, thanking Him for your every breath and boldly asking Him to show you His strength in the middle of your struggle.

If You're Never Mistaken for an Angel, You're Doing It Wrong

Don't forget to be kind to strangers, for some who have done
this have entertained angels without realizing it!

—Hebrews 13:2, TLB

There's no use doing a kindness if you do it a day too late.

—Charles Kingsley

The first order of business in trying to save Jude's life was the surgical implantation of an amnioport in Kelli's abdomen. This device provided a way to supply the baby with fluid that his kidneys, had they been functioning, would have provided on their own.

So a short time after showing up at Cincinnati Children's Hospital, meeting with the team of doctors, and learning what to expect in the coming weeks and months, Kelli was prepped for surgery.

The risk of making an incision into the uterus of a pregnant woman is justified only when the alternative is riskier. Kelli was 100 percent committed to doing absolutely anything to give her son a chance at life. She knew the surgery would be painful, leave lifelong scars, and provide only the slimmest chance of improving Jude's condition. Yet she bravely welcomed the chance to help her son and smiled as they wheeled her into the operating room.

We spent the next hours in the purgatory of the hospital waiting room. Josh was already carrying a huge weight of concern for his unborn child, and now his wife was undergoing major surgery, which added more stress. We prayed. Drank stale coffee. Watched the minute hand crawl across the wall clock. Asked at the desk for an update. Checked the time again. And circled back to start the cycle all over.

Finally a nurse motioned for us to follow her to a consultation room, where a doctor quickly joined us. The port had been inserted, and mom and baby were both fine. The great news that the surgery was a success was tempered by the doctor's reminder that this was just one step in a mile-long journey. But still, it was a step.

We waited for Kelli in the recovery room, and when she woke up in the ICU, she felt understandably miserable, particularly because her physical pain was wrapped up with a profound sense of worry over the health of her child. It was a fatiguing start to a lengthy process that still felt surreal to us. We'd been running hard for several days. And slowing down to accommodate a serious medical operation had done nothing to settle emotions that had come unglued from the moment this ordeal began.

CHRIS'S STORY: ARE YOU AN ANGEL?

We believe angels are real and all around us every day, even though we can't see them. The Bible clearly tells us there are times when angels take on human form and intervene in human events, though I'm not sure I've ever encountered an angel. But there have been times when I've experienced the compassion and kindness of people in ways that made me stop and ponder, *Could they have been angels?* My daily prayer is that I'll step out to show others kindness in such a way that just maybe they'll ask themselves the same question: *Did I just encounter an angel?*

A Hug from Heaven

After the doctors finally cleared Kelli for solid food, I hopped up and made a beeline for the hospital cafeteria, knowing a taste of something good would go a long way toward making her feel better. The only thing I wasn't sure about, not being familiar yet with the rhythm of the hospital, was whether the cafeteria would still be open at that time of evening.

Sure enough, as I turned the corner, I noticed they'd already lowered the gate halfway, indicating to folks like me in the outer hallway that the cafeteria would soon close and that they really didn't want us coming in. Let them just finish cleaning up, please, so they could go on home. Or if we must come in, we at least should be quick about it.

Let's see now. What would Kelli like? I quickly located the few options available, trying to make a good decision against the pressure of the ticking clock, knowing I wouldn't be able to run back down for a second look after the gate shut behind me. Cookies and milk, I finally concluded, would be a nice comfort food she'd probably enjoy. So I grabbed a pack of Lorna Doone shortbread cookies from the shelf and a carton of milk from the refrigerated case, then rushed to the checkout stand.

Normally I'm somebody who makes an effort to chat pleasantly with people behind the counter who are helping me check out. I figure they put up with a lot of hurried, dismissive customers all day, and I want to inject a bit of kindness into those brief exchanges. It feels like the least I can do, you know? But in this case, at this moment, I didn't feel much like small talk. I clunked my milk and cookies onto the little conveyor belt and numbly dug my card out of my purse. I never even attempted to make eye contact with the cashier. As soon as the card reader beeped, I snatched my items and turned away. That's when I heard a voice say, "Do you need a hug?"

I assumed the cashier had intended her comment for someone else and started heading to the exit. Then I heard it again. "Do you need a hug?"

I spun around and quickly remembered I was the only person there. Just her and me. And though I was sure I hadn't been crying when I came in, especially not when I'd approached her at the cash register, tears burst from my eyes. I fell into this stranger's arms, weeping. This wasn't a pretty cry. It was deep, heaving sobs from the depths of my soul.

I seriously doubt she was expecting such a gushing, emotional response. Or maybe the signs of distress were already written on my face, even if I couldn't perceive them. It was several minutes before I could pull myself together, but I finally let go and stepped back from her embrace. She didn't ask what was wrong, and I didn't offer any details. I'm not a crier. In fact, my family and friends can probably count on one hand the number of times they've seen me cry. Yet standing there in a place I'd never been, this stranger's hug had left me deeply comforted. Held. Known. I didn't feel the least bit embarrassed, and after I sniffled my way into being able to take normal breaths again, I said to her, "You're an angel, right?"

She smiled and patted me on the arm. Told me she'd be thinking about me. Then off I went with Kelli's milk and cookies, ducking under the half-lowered gate again as I headed back to her hospital room, a little lighter and more relieved.

I know she wasn't an angel but rather a wonderfully perceptive and caring woman reaching out to hug someone who was hurting. At least

I'm pretty sure she wasn't an angel. I have to admit, I'm still not completely certain! Then it hit me. If I'm never mistaken for an angel, I'm doing it wrong.

I ought to see the hurts of others and reach out in kindness in such a way that every once in a while someone will stop and think, at least for a second, *Oh wow—was that an angel?*

Divine Directions

Two months later, Kelli was coming out of surgery again. Only this time it wasn't to install the amnioport but to remove it. She'd given birth to Jude earlier that morning at Good Samaritan Hospital, just minutes from the Cincinnati Children's Hospital NICU, where we planned to be before the day was over. Now she was recovering not only from childbirth but also from this follow-up operation.

Adrenaline had kept us moving, trying to respond to this knife-turn feeling in our stomachs. We were fighting hard to hope that by some miracle we might even yet be able to replace it with elation and relief. But the courage and confidence were draining from our bodies, even as in desperate prayer we sought to keep ourselves afloat. Day turned to dusk, to evening, to night. And still nothing sounded positive about Jude's prognosis.

Then came news that Kelli had been moved to a private room and we were allowed to go see her. Josh, torn, decided to stay behind in the NICU with Jude, while I sprinted off toward the obstetrics wing, pretty sure I knew how to get there. By this time we'd obviously become a lot more acquainted with the layout of the hospital, and I believed I knew a shortcut I could take to this other part of the building.

But apparently I took a wrong turn. And somewhere in the darkened, unused back hallways of a major city hospital, around ten o'clock at night, I found myself searching for a familiar landmark or directional signage that would get me out of this maze and back to Kelli's bedside. *Please, God, help me.*

I wasn't running, but I was walking briskly. And at some point in my confusion, I must have made one of those stop/start motions—you know, where your brain and your body are trying to sync up and communicate. Your forward movement is taking you one direction, but you're simultaneously thinking you should be going the other way.

I rushed past a woman in a hospital uniform mopping the floor. Looking back on it, I realize I should have asked her whether she could steer me in the right direction. I guess I didn't want to be delayed even for the time it would have taken me to stop and listen. As I sidestepped her mop, she looked up from the floor and I heard the words "Do you need a hug?"

What?

What I really needed were directions, of course, and I needed them immediately. I was so exhausted and flustered. But, yes, I suddenly realized that I desperately needed a hug too. I collapsed into her arms, and the tears came, along with deep comfort. I didn't say what was wrong, and she didn't ask. She just absorbed my sobs, explained how to get to the obstetrics unit, and told me everything would be all right.

I walked away in wonder. Twice in two different hospitals, total strangers had reached out to me with radical compassion.

What was going on?

Angels in the Elevator

Jude went to be with the Lord the next day.

This was supposed to be such a joyous new season of adventure. Most parents will tell you that leaving the hospital with a newborn is scary. Only those who have been in Josh and Kelli's place—who have stepped out of the hospital without their precious baby—know what it's like to carry that kind of emptiness in their hearts. We won't attempt to describe what we can't understand.

After they held Jude for the first and last time, Josh and Kelli knew they couldn't return to the labor and delivery wing with all the other new parents and newborns. We slowly walked out of the NICU and headed for the hospital exit. There was nothing else to be done.

We drove them the few short blocks to the hotel where we'd been staying and quickly secured an additional room for them. We'd never created a contingency plan for this scenario. We hadn't even imagined what would be involved. We'd rehearsed every detail for life with Jude but never considered how to live without him. Josh and Kelli were grieving the unimaginable.

After getting them into a hotel room, I numbly tried to think of how to meet their immediate physical needs. Poor Kelli had given birth the day before and was in pain, and they had hardly eaten or slept since Jude's birth.

Our son Steven and his future wife, Caroline, drove up from their college in Nashville as soon as they heard about Jude and helped take care of Kelli and Josh in whatever small ways they could. Early the next morning, I realized I needed to make a quick trip to the drugstore to buy Kelli the supplies that normally would have been provided by the hospital after birth. It was bitterly cold and overcast as I headed outside to the rental car.

The back tire was completely flat.

Whoooo. I heaved an audible sigh, emitting a cloud of steam that curled and slowly evaporated—fitting imagery for what we'd been experiencing and exactly appropriate for what I was feeling at that moment.

Did this really need to be happening right now? On top of everything? I'd been up all night, was running on fumes. And now this. Tugging the collar of my coat tighter around my neck, I squinted to see how the streets lined up, trying to determine whether the drugstore we'd passed on our way over was within reasonable walking distance.

By the time I'd trudged back through the crusty snow, I was freezing cold and emotionally numb. I was in a hurry to get these things to Kelli but ached with my inadequacy to relieve even an ounce of the pain she and Josh were feeling.

After hitting the elevator button, I waited for the doors to open, along with two young women from the cleaning crew who'd walked up in the meantime. We piled in together when the elevator finally arrived, and I backed into one of the far corners, gripping my bags and closing my eyes, wanting to be invisible while sharing an elevator ride for a few floors.

"Do you need a hug?"

My eyes flew open. *Did one of them really just say that? Did she ask if I needed a hug?* Can you imagine what I thought hearing those same words coming at me again, now in another situation? I mean, this wasn't even a hospital, where people expect someone might be upset about something. I sort of laughed, sort of cried, and then could feel the tears spilling out. "Yes," I half whimpered as the doors dinged open where I needed to exit.

They got out too, and for a minute or more, each young lady gave me a tight, strength-inducing hug. I told them my grandson had gone to be with the Lord the day before, and their tears told me they hurt right along with me.

I don't think you'd be surprised if I said I still haven't quite gotten over the kindness of these random strangers. That was pretty crazy, wasn't it? Yes . . . and no. I believe if you could talk to each of them on the phone and tell them how inspired you were by what they did for me, they'd say, "Did *what* now?" I bet they wouldn't even remember. It likely didn't even register. The hugs they gave were a huge gift to me but probably not a big deal to them.

LOOK BENEATH THE SURFACE

You pass her in the bread aisle, seeing her give a soft squeeze to one or two of the twist-tied bags containing the multigrain variety, checking to be sure they're nice and fresh.

Or you spot him scanning the numbers underneath the carry-on compartments in the airplane, pausing near the place where you're already settled into your aisle seat. You stand uncomfortably to let him wriggle past you, mutter a brief "Excuse me; sorry" before he situates himself in the tight space next to you. It'll likely be all that's said for the duration of the flight, before the two of you nod as you're getting up to leave, wishing each other a silent good day.

Or they file into the row in front of you at church, all six of them, a nice-looking family. Or they fill their tank on the other side of the gas-pump island. Or you see them raking leaves as you drive past their house on your way out of the neighborhood to run some Saturday errands.

Hurting people are everywhere. Do you see them?

Because they're out there.

Do you realize that? Did we recognize that before Jude was born? We understood in general terms that many people in this world are struggling. We knew logically that crises are happening to people every day. Since we are routinely called into situations where others are up against hard places in life, dealing with losses and uncertainties and other shocks to their system, we knew how to recognize people in pain.

But in many ways—for us—it took the experience of being the ones who were hurting to understand pain on a visceral level, to comprehend its silent ache. Until we were the ones who were out shopping for necessities in an unfamiliar city, walking the streets while talking on our cell phones, or trying to figure out what to eat for dinner each night, we didn't realize just how invisible a hurting person can be. If people knew, they would be more caring, patient, and considerate. If people noticed, they might feel compelled to stop and listen, to ask what they can do, to see whether someone wants to talk or needs a hug.

But they *don't* see, usually. They *don't* know. At least we didn't. Most people aren't focused and alert. They aren't aware of others in need among their friends, family, acquaintances, and even the everyday cast of complete strangers.

Maybe it's because most people are struggling so hard underneath their own loads of pain or dread or unsettledness. Or maybe it's because, like ours, their schedules have turned almost every activity into a dead sprint against time. The objectives of each day take supreme importance and simply don't leave allowance for what might be most important to others.

But once you've been there—once you've nearly swooned under the accumulated stress that can complicate even the most routine of daily tasks—you know you're not the only one. Many others, you now realize, have been cycling laboriously through the motions all around you, on days when *you* were the one a little irritated at their slowness and indecision, when *you* were the one a little put off by their haggard appearance.

When you have been that hurting person, it really changes your awareness and capacity for grace. You realize now that you will pass no

fewer than a half-dozen people today in any public place or private setting, whether at work or church or school or any of the places you go,
who are carrying more than they think they can manage.

It's just true. We get it now. We never know who's dealing with what,
except that they're dealing with a lot. And they're *there*. They're *right
there* in front of us—people who are *not* having a good day today.

What do we intend to do about it?

It's easy to say we care about others. Easy to think of ourselves as
basically caring people. But compassion is specific, not general. Compassion is individual, face-to-face action, loving the person who's directly in
front of you. Compassion comes down to changing how you actually act
toward others, not just how you think you should live now or when
you're not quite so busy. It's easy to think of ourselves as being basically
kind. But don't fool yourself. If you can't name a specific instance when
you've shown spontaneous kindness to someone this week, you're probably not an especially kind person. We all have plenty of opportunities to
show kindness and compassion. We just choose not to take advantage of
them.

A one-day mindset will change many things about your life, many
deep and wonderful things. But one of the most radical is discovering a
renewed desire to be a living source of grace and peace to everyone you
meet. Begin to think about how you can show someone kindness today.
It's not about showing kindness *someday;* it's about showing kindness
every day.

SIMPLE KINDNESS

Just imagine what your life would be like if you went into each new day
scanning for people in varying degrees of pain and became an instrument

of compassion in their lives. You may be thinking, *That's too much work for me. I don't have that kind of time, energy, discernment, quick response . . . whatever.* Maybe it just feels like too big a thing.

Well, before Cincinnati we thought we had a good handle on what was big and what was little, in terms of caring for other people. Big things were likely to take a lot of time, cost a lot of money, require a lot of planning, and be a significant inconvenience in general. Our big "aha" was discovering that what's small to us could be big to somebody else—like those people at the cafeteria, hospital, and hotel who took simple actions that had a profound impact on Chris. Their acts of kindness didn't require any money, special equipment or training, or preparation. But despite their relatively small and spontaneous actions, they absolutely blew her away. She felt cared for by them, loved by God, and buoyed in her faith that everything was indeed going to be all right. Their little bit of kindness said a lot.

We realize now that we've missed out on many opportunities through the years to be kind to others because we were waiting until we could do the big thing, make the grand gesture, or purchase something that would wow others with our level of concern.

Then we think about the nurses in the hospital who stopped by Josh and Kelli's room a couple of days before Christmas with a little beat-up cardboard box of decorations. They'd taken them from their break room, and instead of throwing them away or tossing them back in the closet for next year, they shared them with us for a few days. It was just a strand or two of old tinsel and a string of lights—things we could've picked up for nothing at the dollar store, if we'd wanted to or thought about it. Yet they brightened and brought cheer into that little room as if they had been handpicked for the space—some of the most beautiful Christmas decorations we've ever seen.

This was simply another sparkle of grace and blessing that cost little except the effort of being mindful of another's need. It did cost those nurses something else, however—the thing that kindness and compassion *always* cost: risk. Reaching out, even in small ways, never fails to invite the possibility of being rejected.

We don't want to minimize the element of awkwardness that's potentially involved when we try to help those who are hurting, nor are we negating the wisdom of imposing healthy boundaries where needed. But rather than closing off our hearts to others because of the risk to our sense of decorum, shouldn't we be troubled by the idea that people traveling along our path today who *could be* encouraged by our kindness might walk into the night thinking they're all alone in their suffering?

Think about what this one-day philosophy could mean for you. Imagine how meaningful it could be to offer a simple smile to a person in line or a few extra dollars in a tip or an invitation to coffee to a co-worker or neighbor. These might seem like such little things, but there's actually no such thing as a little thing done in love.

Just be sure you don't think of yourself as being unable or unqualified. The people who offered Chris a hug weren't employed in occupations the world considers valuable: they were a lunch lady, a late-shift custodian, the cleaning staff at a chain hotel. They may not have been seen as powerful or important in the world's eyes, but to her they were royalty who made her feel as if she were being comforted by the King of kings.

We may not possess anything in terms of style or status, but hurting people will accept our genuine expression of concern when we offer it. They'll be amazed that somebody picked up on their needs and was willing to let them know they mattered.

People you know, as well as people you *don't* yet know—if you're looking for them—will become visible as the Holy Spirit helps you look beneath the surface and see.

AN ANGEL'S ASSIGNMENT

We recently invited our friends' kids over to our house after school. Max, their second grader, came running in the door, talking at full tilt. "There was this girl today. In the car pool line. And she wanted this person to sit by her. And I let him sit by her. So that was my thing."

Okay, were we supposed to know what he was talking about? He'd told us there was a girl in a car pool line, mentioned what she wanted, and, strangest of all, finished with "So that was my thing."

What thing?

When asked to slow down and repeat his story, he continued after a deep inhale, "There was this girl, see"—still not really pausing much for our comprehension—"in the car pool line . . ."

All right, maybe we'd better just interpret it for you, save us all some time. Max gave up his rightful spot in the car pool line to make a little girl happy. Instead of making it an issue or causing any sort of dustup, Max had scooted over and given the girl her way. That was his "thing," he said.

We realized Max was giving us a report that was expected of him each day. Before he could run off to play, he had to identify this "thing" he had done to be kind to someone else.

And that was it. At his wise parents' insistence, Max had to work each day on a struggle he was experiencing in the kindness department by being sure he intentionally did something nice for someone else. Just one thing.

And we thought, *wow*—what if somebody would hold *us* to that kind of accountability? What if by sundown every day, someone was expecting a report on one act of kindness we'd done for another person? How many afternoons would we come home with something to share?

Would we be like Max and make it our final act of the day? The car pool line was sort of his last chance. He'd already gone through all his classes, his recess, his lunch period, everything, and now he was down to the wire, looking for *any* opportunity to act kindly that might present itself. If we were under the same orders and pressure, don't you think there'd be a real uptick in the nice deeds we did late in the day? We'd be needing to find somebody—quick!—or else we'd be getting no dessert after supper.

It's probably a little childish to think this way. In some cases a simplistic approach like this could feed an old religious tendency to equate performance with spirituality, making us feel bound by duty more than love. But we can see value in planning, each day, not only to be kind when there is a suitable opening but also to find a way to be kind to someone no matter what . . . to go out *looking* for it, not just waiting for it.

Because if Max can do it, we can do it too.

LOVE FIRST

The Bible says, "We know and rely on the love God has for us" (1 John 4:16). We know He loves us because He's given us grace, paid for by the blood of Christ "in accordance with his pleasure and will" (Ephesians 1:5). Our heavenly Father *wanted* to show kindness to us, we've been told, in our broken and helpless condition, "to the praise of his glorious grace, which he has freely given us in the One he loves" (verse 6), His only Son. He didn't wait to be asked; He just made a way. Because "God is love" (1 John 4:16).

Therefore, it's our job—as people who've received such incredible, unexpected, completely undeserved love from God—to let this fountain of love spill over and flow out of us as we move through each day. John said, "This is how love is made complete among us . . . : In this world we are like Jesus" (verse 17). By being love toward others, we dispense His grace and peace into other people's lives, based on the grace and peace He's given us in such fullness.

That's why there's "no fear in love," according to the next verse. "Perfect love"—the kind of love God has given to us—"drives out fear" (verse 18). If we just err on the side of love in trying to determine whether to say something to someone or write him a note or pay for her lunch or whatever, we'll be fine. Love First—that's become our motto. Instead of being too passive, afraid we'll intrude or look funny or not come up with the perfect answer, we'll make mistakes from loving, from loving *first*. We're going to intentionally *love first* today.

John continued in verse 20, "Whoever does not love their brother and sister, whom they have seen, cannot love God, whom they have not seen." His love for us will help us see the unseen so that others will see—in us—the love of God, who is unseen. Beautiful.

If we are doing this right, if we're out there every day being kind to others and showing concern for them, we ought to be mistaken for angels many times throughout our lives. People ought to wonder where this person came from who saw something in the expression on their faces, heard the frustration in their voices, or recognized in their demeanors the pain they were going through and didn't just overlook it like everybody else. We believe God will put us in the exact place where we can be a refreshing cup of grace at precisely the moment when others need it the most.

Love *first*. Grace *first*. Kindness and compassion *first*. No one will be expecting these responses from you. They'll be trying to keep their hurt inside where nobody else suspects it. But if you start each day—each *one day*—with your eyes open to recognize others' pain, you'll see it. You'll see it *everywhere.* In just about everyone. And it won't take much—your act of love and kindness can be so amazingly small and simple—for you to become an enormous gift of grace and peace.

Living the Lesson

If You're Never Mistaken for an Angel, You're Doing It Wrong

Have you ever experienced God's love and kindness through the actions of a stranger? How did that make you feel?

God never wastes a hurt. The pain He allows in our lives can make us more attuned to the pain of others. How have your pain and problems made you more sensitive to people who are hurting?

Read 1 John 4:11–21. List some specific ways you can demonstrate God's love for you by reaching out in love to your friends, family, and neighbors.

Remember that everyone you meet has a hidden hurt. What are some ways you can be more aware of the needs of others today?

Ask God to open your eyes today to see an opportunity to be mistaken for an angel by someone who is in need. Risk loving first! At the end of the day, write down what happened. Do you think you would have acted differently if you hadn't been alert and ready to be used by God? Why or why not?

Hard Isn't the Opposite of Good

Rest, everything's coming together; open your hearts, love is on the way!

—JUDE 1:2, MSG

The ultimate measure of a man is not where he stands in moments of comfort and convenience but where he stands at times of challenge and controversy.

—MARTIN LUTHER KING JR.

Long before we learned Josh and Kelli's pregnancy was potentially in trouble, we completely believed in the goodness of God. It's why we had no hesitation whatsoever praying passionately, trustingly, that He would work a miracle, that He would rescue Jude from what everyone was telling us was the longest of long shots. God is good. We were sure of it! We couldn't think of even one reason that what we wanted wasn't the best plan. So He would want that for us, wouldn't He? He would hate seeing one of our children—one of *His* children—go through the grief of losing their first child.

But here's what Jude taught us: you can't judge God's goodness based solely on whether He's giving you what you want. Being parents ourselves, we know that if our kids asked us for something that was within our power to give and we withheld it despite their pleas that this was *really, r-e-a-l-l-y* important to them, it wouldn't be because we enjoyed hurting them. As all parents know, it would be because we realized something they weren't able to see yet. Parents often possess a wider view than the narrow scope of their children's requests, even if their kids are thoroughly convinced in the moment that they simply can't live without whatever they're wanting.

We get that.

However, here's what we didn't get before Jude—at least not to the extent that we get it now: We'd prayed for something we deeply wanted, believing that Scripture invited us to ask for it, coming boldly to His throne, seeking mercy. We'd felt totally right in making our need known to Him through our many tearful, pleading words. And after all that, He didn't give us what we asked for.

But . . .

He did give us a lot of other things.

A lot of truly *good things.*

If one of those things hadn't been the fresh awareness of what it means to walk with Him in one-day wonder at what He is always doing for us, we don't think we'd have recognized God's goodness. Nothing in Jude's story, all by itself, was making a good case for it. Yet even though Jude is in heaven with the Lord instead of here with us, we've never believed more fully that God is 100 percent good.

CHRIS'S STORY: IT'S WHAT THE LORD GAVE

I frequently go to Haiti, where our church leads an outreach called Farmer Field Schools. We help impoverished families by teaching them sound farming principles, providing them with the tools they need for ending the cycle of hunger.

The training is pretty fascinating, especially for someone like me (I can hardly keep our shrubbery alive). Recently I was in Haiti with our team, which included Dr. Appollo, a Kenyan horticulturist who oversees the entire program for us in Haiti and who is as inspiring as the knowledge he shares.

I clearly recall standing with him in the middle of a village field, kicking at a hardened clod of dry, rocky dirt at my feet. "Is this good land?" I asked him, feeling fairly sure I already knew the answer to my question. I mean, I'm 100 percent on board with the goals of this farming project. I love how it puts food on families' tables, how it restores dignity to people's lives, how it makes the gospel abundantly real to struggling communities. But trying to plant crops on this piece of dry, rocky ground we were given to work with looked like a mistake waiting to happen. "Is this a good plot for us?" is what I was asking. "Does it make sense to plant here?"

"Is this good soil?"

"It is good," he answered instantly, without even looking at where my toes were pointing. "*Of course* it's good," he said. "It's what the Lord gave."

As if that was that.

Because . . . maybe it is.

Maybe the circumstances that look so dark or difficult that nothing will grow from them besides weeds and disappointment might actually surprise us one day with what God intended for them. Maybe the only thing we need to know about our rockiest, most impossible problems is that they are happening within a day the Lord has graciously given to us and therefore are occurring within the context of His goodness.

"This is the day the LORD has made" (Psalm 118:24, NLT). This is the day the Lord has given you. And because it is from the Lord, we know there is goodness in it. Not everything in it will be good. In fact, there most likely will be bad things, painful things—but God can bring good out of that which is not good.

I often go back to that Bible passage from the book of Jude that our daughter texted to us not long after our Jude went to heaven. Just after it says, "Relax, everything's going to be all right," the passage goes on to say, "Rest, everything's coming together" (1:2, MSG).

Did you get that? We can rest in God's goodness because everything is coming together just the way God planned. Maybe right now I can't see the final picture because the puzzle pieces are still being fit together. God is still writing the story, and I'm so close to it that I can't step back and get the eternal perspective.

Not long before we found out Jude was sick, the Lord in His timing (His *good* timing) had drawn some of my Bible study attention to the book of Joshua, especially to that scene following Israel's entrance into the Promised Land when they set up the twelve memorial stones—their *stones of remembrance*.

Maybe you recall the setting. Moses, their great and longtime leader, had recently died. The last of the unfaithful generation who'd been wandering in the wilderness for close to forty years were exiting the stage. God had established Joshua as the man to guide the nation forward, and the Israelites promised that this time they would not be afraid to go for it. Instead of turning back in fear as their forefathers had done, instead of quivering at the challenges awaiting them in Canaan, they approached the banks of the Jordan River and prepared to forge across.

But God wanted to show them the strength He'd provide in this new, dangerous territory they were entering. So instead of having them brave the current as best they could, He commanded the waters of the southerly flowing Jordan to dam up against an invisible wall somewhere to the north—think Red Sea 2.0—and allowed them dry passage into their destiny.

Pretty cool.

A really *good* thing God did for them.

Once they'd made it across, the Lord commanded Joshua to choose twelve men—one from each of the tribes of Israel—to walk back into that dry riverbed, select a sizable rock, and hoist it up onto their shoulders. Then those twelve strong guys marched those twelve big rocks into the Israelite camp on the Promised Land side of the Jordan. They stacked them in a pile. And Joshua said to the people, "In the future when your descendants ask their parents, 'What do these stones mean?' tell them, 'Israel crossed the Jordan on dry ground.' For the LORD your God dried up the Jordan before you until you had crossed over" (4:21–23).

Stones of remembrance.

You know why we need them? Because we forget even the *big* things. The monumental things. Over time, we lose the context and wonder—the genuine miracle, really—of what God has done in our lives.

Since we can forget even the major things, things that at the time were so massively front and center, so ridiculously good—so indicative of God's goodness toward us—what should we expect to happen to the *little* things once they trickle past us? Is it possible to remember them? To tell our kids about them? Will we still be raving about them in years to come?

Will we even notice them as they're happening?

When our family started walking into this crisis season, I made a decision right from the start. The medical professionals who were informing and advising us about Jude's condition were making it clear that the good news we all wanted was probably not going to happen. There was almost no reason to believe, except through the eyes of purely audacious faith, that Jude would be able to survive what he was dealing with.

But I wrote something down as I was praying into that cold reality. There at the outset, I said, "God, I want to watch for what You do and not just focus on the tough stuff." I knew we would be confronted with all kinds of dark moments in the days ahead when it would be hard to see His goodness or hear His voice. But I was determined that even if the big things—most notably, the *biggest* thing—did not go as we hoped, I would refuse to miss seeing God's goodness in the midst of it.

Because I knew it would be there.

I just needed to watch for it.

Love Is on the Way

When you're going through pain, just trying to make it through the day, it feels so hard. It's so easy to close your eyes and your heart to the goodness God wants to bring into your life. When I start to go down this road, that passage in Jude always comes back to me: "Open your hearts, love is on the way!" (1:2, MSG).

When we're suffering, we want to close off our hearts to God and others because we're afraid of being hurt again. But if I open my heart and my eyes in faith, I'll start to see that love is on the way and God's love is all around me.

When I live with my heart partially closed off, I can miss recognizing and receiving the love and goodness God is trying to give me.

I admit it's scary to live with a heart wide open, especially when you've been wounded. Let's be honest. It's a huge risk to live with a wide-open heart because, yes, you will be hurt at times.

It may not be a risk to live with your heart closed off, but that's because you're guaranteed to miss out on the blessings and love that are meant for you. When you open your eyes and start looking for God's goodness in small ways, God starts opening your heart to experiencing His goodness in big ways. Today, ask God to open your eyes to His goodness all around you.

If you expect God's goodness, you'll start experiencing God's goodness in a fresh and powerful way. Open your heart today. Love is on the way!

Don't Forget to Remember

Most of us tend to narrate our lives in terms of the story lines playing out at any given moment. Maybe it's sports season for you right now, and your kids are involved in extra activities. Maybe you're going through an exceptionally busy period at work, and you're in the midst of a big project that's occupying a lot of your time. Maybe you're in the middle of a move—organizing the endless details, the paperwork, the timing of buying and selling and packing and paying. I don't know what you're facing. But if somebody asked you what was going on in your life today, your answer, if you felt like getting into it, would probably involve your current list of activities, both the good and the not so good. We think our actions are our story. That's the story we *think* we're telling.

In fact, what we're living out each day are our *relationships* with the Lord. All the other things—the struggles and the successes, even your weekend plans and the fun stuff—are the scenery, the backdrop against which the real story of your life is being told. The larger narrative is always what's happening between you and God and how your relationship with Him is either growing or receding—developing either more closeness or more distance, more freedom or more distrust—within the context of this particular stage of your life.

So think with me for a minute about how relationships work—

whether it's a marriage, friendship, or relationship between parent and child. You can probably recall a number of big moments or markers that have contributed to the overall character of your relationships. In reflecting on some of the most important people in your life, perhaps you could point to a few major events—equivalent to the Jordan River crossing—that have helped create the shared lore of those relationships.

But those moments are the exceptions. They're not really what fosters the tenderness or strength of your personal bond. Relational trust is built not on the basis of two or three unforgettable days but on those hundreds and thousands of ordinary days when you have demonstrated love and care for each other. It turns out that the little things *are* the big things.

Think of the person you trust most in this world. Based on all your hundreds or thousands of interactions with this individual, if you found yourself facing a significant challenge, how quickly would you turn to him for help? How confidently would you reach out to him? And how would you expect him to respond to you? With coldness and indifference? Or with focused love and attention? With goodness?

When someone has been faithful over and over again—and you've seen it, felt it, and frequently thanked her for it—you don't need her to part the Jordan River this afternoon to convince you that you can trust her. You already know it. You know her heart. You already believe in her goodness. You've been keeping tabs on forgettable things that by their sheer quantity are able to far outweigh even the unforgettable things.

Our relationships with the Lord are the same. The everyday moments, the easy-to-overlook moments, are actually what cement our relationships with God. If you're up against something hard or worrisome today and you don't know whether God is good enough to want to hear you or answer you or care about what you're enduring and needing, could I possibly convince you to do what we did? Find something to write on or in. Any old notebook or piece of scratch paper will do. If in a day's time you haven't cataloged for yourself a few fresh reminders of God's goodness that have been escaping your notice and that might just redeem your trust in His love for you, I'll be very surprised.

I understand if you're skeptical that something so simple could make any difference. Maybe to you this smacks of head games, a sanctified form of self-talk. Maybe it's all a bit too sweet sounding for your taste. Yet the reason it's so powerful is precisely because of the harshness of our reality. Each of us is *desperate* for God's goodness. We completely depend on Him not only for His presence but also for confidence in His good intentions.

If life were a Hallmark movie, sure, maybe we could treat this cataloging of His daily kindness as if it were all pajamas and hot chocolate and soft Christmas music playing in the background. But being aware of what God is doing in our lives every day is essential to our hope and well-being, and it adds renewed vitality to our relationships with Him.

If His goodness were only a bonus—if it were capable only of taking our lives from maybe an eight to a nine—then we could afford to schedule this exercise once every few months. But tell me: Does your life sometimes just barely make it into positive numbers? Then if you're not convinced *every day* of God's goodness—and are recording it, along with the date and time, somewhere you can see it—you might not be able to keep your head above zero.

I remember reading in the book of Psalms one morning while we were in Cincinnati, and I came across this incredible verse that spoke directly to what my heart was feeling: "When my soul is in the dumps, I rehearse everything I know of you" (42:6, MSG).

Listen, my soul was definitely "in the dumps" that day. My reserves were running low. I was tired. I was discouraged. My arms felt almost pulled out of their sockets, sore from reaching up for hope and reaching down to help.

But the writer said that "when my soul is in the dumps," I should do what?

"Rehearse." Rehearse what?

"Everything I know of you."

And that's exactly what I did. If I hadn't had a ready-made way of doing it, I don't know where I would have started. But on that cold morning, I picked up our well-worn Miracle Book and started rehearsing. Rehearsing His praises. Remembering the goodness of the Lord.

All I can tell you with certainty as I sit here flipping through Jude's Miracle Book today is that in rereading and remembering, I am never not amazed at how good our God is. I can recall instantly the place where I was sitting when I wrote each entry and from there remember the place where each occurrence actually happened. Reading this book is tinged with an ache, of course, because it so vividly captures a time when we still had hope that the exact miracle we wanted was out there in front of us, that this was what God was leading us toward with each new evidence of His goodness.

But now that I see it from my current vantage point, I can understand something else: it was *all* a miracle. Every little thing was a miracle. Every single day. And so is *this* day that is waiting in front of me now. You and I are surrounded by God's goodness, whether we know it or not.

Hard Isn't the Opposite of Good

Reflect on a hard time in your past. Have you experienced any positive character changes that came out of that season or situation?

Read Joshua 4:21–23. Why is it important to remember the good things God does for us?

Read Psalm 42:6 (MSG). In the space below, record (or rehearse) everything you know about the Lord and His goodness.

How have you witnessed God's goodness in your life in the past week? Make a list in the space below.

It's so easy to close off our hearts to God when we're hurting and miss the blessings He has for us. Write a prayer asking God to help you open your heart today and be ready to receive His goodness.

Everyone Needs a Miracle Book

Open my eyes so I can see what you show me of your miracle-wonders.

—Psalm 119:18, msg

The sacred moments, the moments of miracle, are often the everyday moments, the moments which, if we do not look with more than our eyes or listen with more than our ears, reveal only . . . the gardener, a stranger coming down the road behind us, a meal like any other meal. But if we look with our hearts, if we listen with our whole being and our imagination . . . what we may see is Jesus himself.

—Frederick Buechner

W hen our kids were growing up, their favorite place, their dream place to go on vacation, was Disneyland. For them, and now for our grandchildren, it really is "the happiest place on earth." For us, it feels more like "the most expensive place on earth!" But we have to say we love it too.

After our family's first trip to Disneyland, our kids became avid hidden–Mickey Mouse hunters. In case you didn't know, the architects of Disney theme parks have subtly incorporated Mickey's iconic ears throughout the parks. They may be stitched into a Disney hotel carpet design or etched into a concrete wall on the side of a theme-park building, but you would never notice them unless you were specifically looking for them. Once our competitive children started searching, they began to see them everywhere and tried to find more than their siblings by the end of the day.

Seeing miracles of God in your life is a little bit like watching for hidden Mickeys. Once you start looking for them, you'll begin to see them, and then you'll wonder why you were so blind to them before. God's miracles are all around us. They are stitched into the most un-expected circumstances and etched into the most unlikely people.

A big part of following God's word from Jude is opening your eyes so you'll recognize God's love. When you recognize His love, you're a lot more likely to open your heart and receive it. That's where a miracle book comes in. When you choose a simple journal and decide you're going to watch for God working in your life and write down what He's doing, you take a step of faith that says, *God, I'm expecting Your goodness today in my life.* Here's the thing: Don't try to write your thoughts down perfectly for the world to see. Just write them down imperfectly but from your heart.

Hidden Miracles

It was really just a moleskin journal that we already had. Blank pages. Anything would've sufficed. We grabbed it sometime during the dark night following Jude's initial twenty-week scan. But every night after that, within the close quarters of our living conditions in Cincinnati, part of our routine was to share our memories of the day and ask each other, "What have we got for the Miracle Book today?"

The book you're reading right now is in many ways the fruit of how we answered that daily question. We've already told you, of course, how this story ends. But Jude's Miracle Book (and the subsequent volume we filled up) is proof that Jude's story was actually only beginning. Even now, people come up to us on a regular basis to tell us how Jude has changed their lives. That's honestly no exaggeration. Because God's daily miracles are happening all around us all the time. God was working then in the saddest, most stressful situation we'd ever experienced. And He's working now in the midst of whatever you're going through.

When people talk about the way Jude changed their lives, they're actually saying *God* changed their lives and is continuing to change their lives. He is helping them become increasingly aware of His everyday goodness. And He used one little boy to do it.

He chooses to use what the world sees as insignificant to reveal His power.

In one sense, we were just trying to figure out what people are supposed to do when their child or grandchild is critically ill. It was all so new to us and to Josh and Kelli. But even when our eyes were focused on working step by step within the medical process to bring Jude safely into the world, the Lord was accomplishing something so much bigger than our single-minded goal, despite how fervently and ferociously we wanted it.

God was taking us through a tough season, and He knew that when we came out on the other side, we wouldn't be holding the grand prize we desperately wanted. He knew that. And He wanted to protect us. So He made sure we didn't leave with nothing. He made sure our hearts, so terribly empty, would still be filled.

We would be filled with memories of His goodness. Memories of His daily miracles.

Most of them, yes, were little things. Little kindnesses offered. Little bursts of strength. Little moments of opportunity that occurred only because we were away from home, encountering people and situations we never would have otherwise. But here's the truth: you and I have no real idea what constitutes a big thing or a little thing, any more than we know why one family receives the answer to their prayer and another one doesn't. It's not really our role to judge within the broad scope of life.

But everything is ours to *remember*. And if we don't do it every day—or at least as a matter of prayerful habit—we'll forget. We'll bowl right over these little miracles. We'll stay consumed by whatever is hitting us next. We'll fix our attention on whatever is loudest or bossiest or most pressing. And we'll miss what is so easy to overlook: the goodness of God, the little miracles He's doing.

We don't have any doubt you could fill a book with these as well.

THE BELIEVING BUTCHER

Bishop Philip Kitoto and his wife, Dinah, are dear friends of our family and trusted mentors of ours from Nairobi, Kenya. They lead a great ministry and have trained thousands of young leaders throughout Africa to make a difference in their communities. We have found that in the most difficult times of our lives, Philip and Dinah have been there to show us compassion and to share wisdom from God that speaks directly to what we are going through.

Not long after we arrived in Cincinnati, Philip called Josh to check in and encourage him and Kelli as they walked this faith journey. He said he'd been praying and the Lord had shown him something he wanted to share.

"Just picture the butcher"—imagine these words being spoken in his lovely, warm Kenyan accent.

Picture the butcher who does not know the Lord. What does he
do? He slaughters his goat in the morning, and he does not know

if anyone will come past and buy it. Yet he's already made preparation—by faith—and then he waits for a customer. If no one comes, the meat will spoil and his income will be lost. What great faith he shows!

Or picture the hotel owner who also doesn't know the Lord. What does he do? He makes up all his beds in the morning, not knowing if anyone will arrive to stay in his rooms. If no travelers come, he will have no income. Yet he prepares for them and waits. What great faith!

Yet if the butcher who doesn't know the Lord is willing to slaughter his goat in the morning without seeing his business yet transacted, and if the hotel owner who doesn't know the Lord is willing to prepare a room for someone he doesn't yet see, do they have more faith than we do? Do they have more faith than a believer in God?

We have a good Father. We are taking no risks by putting our confidence in His love and strength and provision. We're playing no odds; we're facing no possibility that He won't come through for us, in His own wise and life-giving way. He may not intervene in the way we'd hoped or expected. Our prayer and His answer may not match up. But He will see our faith, and He will know we are trusting Him.

Get up in the morning and get believing.

There's an old saying: "If you pray for rain, carry an umbrella." A personal miracle book is your umbrella. It's your statement of faith to God that you are expecting rain. You are expecting an outpouring of His blessings on your life.

When you write down the lessons God is teaching you and the miracles He is doing in your life, you're choosing to remember His goodness.

In remembering what God did, you are also allowing yourself to feel the pain of remembering—the sadness, the trial, the hurt that you were going through at the time. But the pain of remembering is worth the joy of trusting. By faith you are stating, "God's gifts are perfect, so my understanding is flawed. Today I don't understand. Today I'm confused. But one day it will all be clear. Until then I'll trust in the goodness of the God who loves me."

CELEBRATE THE CURRENT SEASON

One of the most perspective-changing aspects of having a personal miracle book is that it helps you celebrate in the middle of stressful seasons in your life. By the way, every season is stressful, but it's also joyful! The problem is we rarely stop to celebrate the season we're in because we're looking forward to the next season of life that won't be "as stressful."

If you don't learn to celebrate the season you're in, you'll never celebrate. Life is made up of many seasons, but it's our human nature to think that the season we're currently in is the most difficult.

When you're a teenager, you can't wait until you're on your own and can do whatever you want to do. You think, *If I could just get out from under my parents' authority, life would be great.*

Then you graduate from high school and go off to college or start a career and realize, *Whoa! This responsibility stuff is hard! What I really need is someone to share life with. A soul mate. When I get married, everything will be perfect.*

Then you get married, and it turns out your spouse has flaws you never saw. And the discovery that life is no longer about you at every moment but is now about "we" is a huge and difficult change.

So you start thinking, *I know what would fix our troubles. A baby.*

Now, that will change everything. And it does. You have a baby, and within a few days you're thinking, *If I could just string together six hours of sleep, life would be good.*

Then you start to dream about when the kids are old enough to put food in their own mouths. They start to grow, and it's not long before you're stepping in apple juice and there are crayon marks all over the walls and it's too crazy to go to a restaurant anymore. And you think, *When the kids start school, everything will settle down.*

Before you know it, the kids are in school, and you're driving them around all day to their lessons and practices, you're up to your knees in dirty laundry, and you have to stay up late helping them with homework. Then you think, *I can't wait until they can drive! That will really alleviate a lot of my stress.*

Then they are driving, and you're dealing with really serious stuff, and you find out raising teenagers is more difficult than you ever dreamed. So you think, *When they graduate! Yes! Then everything will be great!*

Soon they graduate and go their own ways, and you hit that empty-nest stage and start thinking, *If only I could just have them as babies again. Wouldn't that be wonderful!*

What is it that keeps us focused only on the tough stuff in the season we're in and makes us want to rush through it? The truth is, every season of life has its pain and stress but every season is also filled with miracles and great joy.

We have found it all comes down to a daily choice. What are we going to focus on in this season? The Miracle Book has helped us focus on the miracles in the middle of the mess.

We have now been through all the seasons of life we just outlined, and in our experience, they were all way harder than we imagined *and* way more glorious than we could have ever dreamed. That's why we have to choose to celebrate the season we're in. Otherwise, we'll see only the problems and pain and miss out on the beauty of today.

Kris and Jessica are some friends of ours who were so affected by Jude's story that they decided to become foster parents in the hope of adopting a child. They are currently fostering a little boy whom they already love dearly. Of course, things could completely change any day. The birth mother's custody could be reinstated without warning. Really, all Kris and Jessica want for this little one is what's best for him, and they're committed to loving him fiercely as long as he is in their care, whether that's for a week or a lifetime.

Kris told us recently, "Jessica and I are praying a 'just for today' prayer like Jude taught us. *Lord, just for today give us the ability to love this little boy in a way that he'll experience Your love.*" He went on to say, "Really, none of us are promised tomorrow. So we'll celebrate the miracle of this little boy today!"

We encourage you to start celebrating God's goodness by starting your own miracle book today. Every time you read it, God will open your eyes to see how much He loves you.

Don't wait until you have time to write down your thoughts as beautifully and brilliantly as C. S. Lewis did; just pick up a pen and begin. Either you'll capture thoughts imperfectly or you'll lose them. If you let a lack of time or talent prevent you from doing this, you may never do it. But if you discipline yourself to write down your thoughts imperfectly so you won't lose them, you can go back and read them to remember God's goodness in your life. Open your eyes today and watch for miracles. Open your journal tonight and start your personal miracle book. When you open your eyes in faith, your eyes will be opened to what God is doing.

Living the Lesson

Everyone Needs a Miracle Book

What big or small miracles have you seen God doing in your life recently?

Colossians 4:2 says, "Devote yourselves to prayer, being watchful and thankful." Are you on the lookout for God's goodness in your life? Could you be missing some of His miracles because you aren't watching for them?

Colossians 4:2 says we're also to be thankful for what God is doing in our lives. Make a list of things you are thankful for in your current season of life.

God works His greatest miracles in our messes. What is an area of your life where you need God's miracle in the middle of the messiness?

Are you keeping up to date in your miracle book? What are you learning by taking the time to record what God is doing in your life?

Share Your Story . . . Even If You Don't Know How It Ends

He comes alongside us when we go through hard times, and before you know it, he brings us alongside someone else who is going through hard times so that we can be there for that person just as God was there for us.

—2 CORINTHIANS 1:4, MSG

What is most universal is most personal.

—HENRI NOUWEN

Wearing black as a symbol of mourning was a commonly accepted (even expected) practice among most people in the West throughout much of the twentieth century. The ritual actually goes back much further in history, but for a long time it was seen as a privilege of royalty and the social elite rather than of the commoner. Widows, in particular, were expected to wear black for up to a year following the death of their husbands and could then begin incorporating somber colors such as gray or purple into their wardrobes after the first year.[5]

We bring this up because for a long time, people didn't have to guess whether people they saw in public had suffered a significant loss and might still be grappling with grief. Their clothing communicated to others on their behalf. People knew they needed to be sensitive around the recently bereaved. No one expected them to be bright and bubbly.

People spoke to them in caring, understanding tones. Perhaps part of what helped those healing from loss were the frequent opportunities to talk about it, since others knew of it without needing to be told. Those who were going through significant seasons of loss were not as hidden and unknown as they are today.

The only modern equivalent might be the way people feel when they see veterans or people in uniform. They tend to want to pay them respect, to express gratitude for their service to our country. All it takes to elicit that response are the clothes they are wearing and other visible evidence of their experiences.

But in general, it's just not possible anymore to easily identify those who grieve. We wonder whether in many cases that fact makes our grief harder to move through. If we're being honest, if we had had a choice, we would have preferred to keep everything about Jude's life and death to ourselves. We needed to talk but didn't know how to start. What we wanted was to retreat, to crawl into a hole somewhere or circle the wagons so that nobody could get in or out. And frankly, as our culture has evolved, particularly in the ways we find community, it can be a whole lot easier now to isolate ourselves than it was in times past.

Do you know what we mean?

Have you ever felt that way?

This is what grief does to most of us. It makes us want to withdraw. It makes us want to shun interaction. It makes us want to pull the blinds, get back into bed, and avoid anything that might be upsetting. More than anything, we don't want to break down emotionally in public, which remains a distinct possibility when a loss is fresh.

But if others knew . . . if others could see . . . if we weren't able to hide away . . .

We'd actually receive a double blessing.

We have come to believe that sharing your story is good for you. By isolating yourself and staying distant from people, you can end up wiping away the good memories you *do* have. You can also strain relationships that would be enormously helpful to you at this critical moment in your life. Although the grieving process looks different for every person, we encourage you not to clam up and avoid talking about your hurts and feelings, even though that sometimes seems easier.

Although sharing your story benefits you, it is also incredibly good for others. There are so many people who need to hear what you have to say, and you will likely be pleasantly surprised by the experiences and commonalities you share. So don't be afraid to invite uncomfortable conversations or let others see your emotions and pain.

We had no idea—*no* idea—that some of the people who approached us after hearing of Jude's death had also lost children or grandchildren or had suffered a miscarriage (or several) and had been dealing with those losses alone. Some of these people we'd known for years, men and women with whom we'd spent lots of time. Yet they carried wounds that a good number of them had rarely shared—not with us anyway.

It's incredible, really, how hard it can be for some of us to share our stories. Often we just don't know how. We're afraid we'll say something wrong. We may not want to make ourselves the main topic of conversation. Or maybe we're not happy with some of the aspects of our stories or the choices we made. Perhaps we'd rather others not hear our stories.

But you never know how your story will affect someone else. Many of the things people shared with us made a remarkable difference, even if they didn't realize it. And I'm sure we haven't thanked them enough, even yet. Often the most pivotal part of what they shared was not any kind of profound discovery or principle but merely a minor detail that no one else but God could know would bring such comfort to us. It was as if in that moment He winked from heaven and said, *See, I'm looking out for you. I sent this person to you to say this to you.* They didn't know it, but we did.

We're well aware that being in the presence of someone in pain can make you feel awkward. You don't know what to say. Are your words too much? Too little? Is the sentiment you wish to share too trite or sappy? But if you look for moments, listen for clues, and are willing to unlock some of your sad memories, your words will blossom into blessing for someone else as God gives you opportunity.

This will be a better use of your grief than surrendering it to silence.

THE LEGACY OF LOSS

Have you ever noticed that many of the stories throughout the Bible are examples of loss?

Adam and Eve lost the Garden of Eden—as did we—when sin entered the world and reduced us to fallen people in need of rescue. This same first family then lost their second son, who was killed by their first-born, a crushing grief that entered their lives sooner than anyone could've expected.

Abraham felt sure he was going to lose Isaac, the child of promise, when God tested his faith by commanding him to sacrifice his son. It was a moment of terror that surely stuck with him through the years, even after being saved from making such an impossible choice.

Jacob lost his beloved wife Rachel in childbirth during their journey away from her father's abusive household. He had loved her enough at first sight to work seven hard years in exchange for her hand and then seven more years when he was tricked into marrying her sister instead.

Joseph lost his home, his family, his roots, and his status as the favored son when his own brothers sold him into slavery. He had to start over in a new nation with nothing but his steadfast faith in God to sustain him.

Moses's mother lost her son when a paranoid Egyptian ruler issued an edict to have all the Hebrew male babies killed. Moses lost his home and position as adopted grandson to the pharaoh, then went on to lose the settled peace and seclusion of a shepherd's life when God called him to a shepherding job far beyond his skill set.

The children of Israel lost the opportunity to enter the Promised Land because of their incessant complaining and lack of confidence in God's good intentions. Then they lost Moses, the only leader they had ever known, in a massive generational turnover.

Saul lost his kingdom when life proved bigger than his character. David lost relationship with most of his family thanks to infighting, distrust, and the fallout of his sin. His son Solomon lost his way as king, succumbing to foreign women instead of relying on his massive God-given wisdom.[6]

And those are just a few of the highlights among many available examples. But as we know, the Bible culminates in the lowest and at the same time highest point of all, when God the Father didn't lose but gave His only Son in fulfillment of His plan and purposes. History divides at a death—the death of Jesus as substitute for our sins.

But is the Bible a sad book? Is the legacy of God's reaching out and redeeming His people from a lost and dying world a sad story, since it's littered with so much sadness and loss?

In reality, these stories give us hope because they connect to our lives and to what we've gone through. These stories speak to the hardships we've endured ourselves. They remind us that death and loss, sin and suffering, hardship and sorrow, struggle and pain are all part of the human experience. None of us is exempt. No period in history has ever been devoid of difficulty. Yet God has always kept His people looking to the death and resurrection of Christ as the reason no grief is ever final.

So be encouraged by these stories of loss, knowing that God did not populate Scripture only with happy, prosperous, intact, unsullied people who make us feel as though we're alone in our pain or as if God doesn't understand it. Instead, the Bible shows us death so that God can show us the triumph of His life. It doesn't skip over the messiness of life as if it doesn't exist. Rather, God chose to include the unwanted and unpleasant in holy Scripture because He is stitching every story, no matter how unresolved, together into the greatest story ever told.

Tell.

Your.

Story.

Unafraid of the Unresolved

Our family decided that as much as it hurt to talk about Jude, we were not going to avoid it, even if we ran the risk of prompting tears or falling to pieces altogether. We weren't going to edit him out of our conversations. His loss was real. Jude was real. Though he is no longer here, we would make sure he was always present in our family. We wouldn't be wearing black, but we would be displaying our grief, and we *would* be talking about Jude.

This position was easier for us to take because we'd been pretty open with others about Jude's situation all along. People knew what was going on. We'd reported some of the details during Kelli's treatments and Jude's hospitalization. This kept us talking about him, and praying with others about him regularly helped a lot. People would often ask us, "How's it going? How's that grandson of yours? How are *you*? How can we help you?" Their prayers and kindnesses—even at times when, to tell you the truth, we might not have felt like talking—were actually all important. They were useful for building our resilience and recovery.

None of that was a surprise to us.

However, the part that became a huge change-of-direction lesson for us—and maybe will be for you also—was that we didn't need to wait for a happy ending before we could talk about our experiences. Our job is not to be God's public relations department, spinning information so that it casts our faith or Him in a better light.

Perhaps you feel the same pressure to hold your cards close to your chest while your current crisis is playing out. Your inclination is to give it time, until things look a lot better. Then your story will be much easier to explain, to package. In the meantime, you can reply to polite inquiries with canned responses suitable for public consumption, such as "I'm fine," "It's all good," or "It's in God's hands. Thanks for asking."

Listen, we're right there with you. We pray that everything bothering you today turns out well. We really do. If you're sorting through an upsetting tangle of delays and questions and problems and unknowns, we hope all is resolved so you have a story where you can say, "Let me tell you how God worked. It was great. It was awesome." That's what *all* of us want—to express our gratitude for the cool things God did.

But don't wait until your story ends to share it. Don't wait to see whether everything turns out okay before you let others in. Of course, it makes sense that you're worried and stressed when things are going badly. Your emotions are probably all over the place, and you may not want others to judge you. But there are always people out there who are in their own messy or painful seasons. Invite them to sit down with you and hear you; bang together on the doors of heaven in prayer. It will do more for *both* of you than your private vigil of desperation.

Waiting for the Lord is one thing—and a *good* thing. Waiting for Him to act while He strengthens you spiritually is a courageous, mature posture for you as a child of God.

But waiting to share your story until you've seen it scrubbed of all the anguish and sweat and unflattering tears is not beneficial. Waiting for full resolution of all your pain is not realistic. Waiting until you're finally the recipient of good news, instead of toiling along in prayerful persiverance, will keep you from sharing your story for a long time in most instances.

What's the matter with being real? What are we really protecting by not sharing with others from our vacuum of pain and need, where our disabilities and deficiencies are the most exposed? What if God will receive maximum glory only if we allow others to see what He's doing right now—with *us,* in *this* situation, when life looks like *this?*

Why not show people our *today,* not just our tomorrow?

That's where real faith is best seen—not in resolved, pretty, buttoned-up stories but in situations that are largely still in process, still murky and incomplete.

Grief, loss, and sadness are among the most personal experiences we encounter in life. No one should ever impose demands on how someone else *should* feel or *should* act or *should* respond. It's none of anyone else's business, really. When you're grieving or struggling, do it your way.

But what we *feel* and what we *need* are often two different things. That's why sometimes we need gentle reminders that help us see a way forward through our loss. That's what sharing does. It gives us a prism of perspective in our grief that can filter light back into our darkness. The stories you share will be the stories that heal.

Living the Lesson

Share Your Story . . . Even If You Don't Know How It Ends

Have you ever lied when someone asked you "How are you doing?" Maybe you were really hurting, but you just said, "I'm great. How about you?" Why do you think it's hard to share our pain and brokenness with others?

Read Psalm 13. In this psalm we see David holding nothing back as he poured out his questions and hurt to God. Do you have trouble pouring out your pain and anger to God? Why or why not?

What aspects of your story or current situation are the hardest for you to share with others?

How are you doing, *really*? Write down the painful realities of your current situation. Thank God that He really does care how you're doing, and ask Him to give you His peace and comfort today.

Ask a friend or family member, "How are you doing, *really*?" Make sure he understands that you honestly want to know how he's doing, and then be willing to open up with him too. Afterward, reflect on your conversation. How did your intentionality make you feel? How did he respond to it? How could you follow up to let him know you really care?

When Nothing Makes Sense, Just Obey

Trust in the Lord with all your heart, and do not trust in your own understanding. Agree with Him in all your ways, and He will make your paths straight.

—Proverbs 3:5–6, NLV

No trumpets sound when the important decisions of our life are made. Destiny is made known silently.

—Agnes de Mille

By God's providence, our friends from Kenya, Philip and Dinah
Kitoto, were speaking at our church the night before Josh and
Kelli headed to Cincinnati. That Sunday night, they gathered with our
family and a few close friends to pray for Josh and Kelli and for the life
of their unborn son, our precious little Jude.

Just before we started to pray, Philip said in his wise and compassionate way, "I'm reminded of Ezekiel in the vision of dry bones, where God
leads Ezekiel to look over a massive valley filled with dried-out human
bones as far as the eye can see. God then says to Ezekiel, 'Son of man, can
these bones live?' And Ezekiel says, 'Sovereign LORD, you alone know.'"
Philip continued, "Do we know if Jude will live? Only You know, sovereign Lord. We trust Jude to our sovereign Lord. But then God told Ezekiel to prophesy life over those bones. And, Josh," he said, looking at Josh

with his winsome and penetrating eyes, "just as Ezekiel's job was to speak life over the dry bones, your job is to speak life over Jude and trust him to our sovereign Lord."[7]

It was a powerful moment.

And Josh totally took it to heart. For the entirety of those nine weeks of waiting, he spoke in faith over Jude each night. He placed his hand along with Kelli's hand on her round, pregnant belly, moving as close to Jude as possible, and prayed for God to bless, heal, and sustain him. The two of them sang songs of praise and heartfelt prayer over their son each night before bed, letting him hear the muffled sounds of worship in his parents' voices.

Was it going to make any difference? Would Jude survive? Could these bones live, as Philip had asked, quoting the Lord's words to the prophet? We didn't know the answer to those questions. Only God knew. But Josh and Kelli's assignment as they entered that dark tunnel of life-and-death difficulty was to trust their God with the life of their son.

To believe.

To have faith.

Faith is not a conditional commitment. Faith is not a wait-and-see game-time decision. Faith is not a contingency plan that we might decide to employ if conditions seem to warrant it. Faith is the preset outlook we bring into every situation, whether it looks like it's going to work out or not.

The thing about faith in God—as opposed to just faith in general—is that it's guaranteed to be recognized by the Lord and to result in a response. That's what the Bible says: "Without faith it is impossible to please God, because anyone who comes to him must believe that he exists and"—here's the part we're not always so sure about—"that he rewards those who earnestly seek him" (Hebrews 11:6).

WHEN IT'S LATER, IT'S GREATER

There's simply no doubt about it. Faith will not end in failure. We may endure days of loss; faith may not prevent us from feeling the weight of heart-crushing trials. But faith will always be rewarded by our Father in heaven. Earnestly seeking Him leads to a guaranteed victory.

Obviously, in many cases our lifetimes on earth may end up being too short for God's victory to become fully visible in a particular area or for our trials to have tidy and instantly positive conclusions. Our days are "a mere handbreadth," David said. "Everyone is but a breath" (Psalm 39:5). We're not promised complete answers to questions that will require the much-larger perspective of eternity to interpret.

But faith is always the right answer anyway. Faith in God is always a strong place to stand. After everything the Lord has done to bring genuine hope into our lives, how could He possibly decide midstream just to shove off and leave us untethered, to leave our faith in Him void and worthless? He will not let something as severe as His own Son's death prove to be a waste of blood and everyone's time. As Josh and Kelli said along the way, they as parents were willing to go to any lengths necessary to try to save and protect their son. Yet God the Father went to even more unthinkable lengths *to do the exact opposite* so that His Son would die because of His love for all of us.

Shouldn't that inspire us to put full stock in our faith?

We are safer in His arms today than any of our feelings might be telling us. Because "no matter how many promises God has made, they are 'Yes' in Christ" (2 Corinthians 1:20). They are as sure as the world. They are *more* sure than the world. As Paul went on to say, "It is God who makes both us and you stand firm in Christ. He anointed us, set his seal of ownership on us, and put his Spirit in our hearts as a deposit, guaranteeing what is to come" (verses 21–22).

God makes sure we "stand firm in Christ" (verse 21).

And we make sure we stand firm "by faith" (verse 24).

Faith is what the day calls for. Faith is what *your* day is calling for, *this* day. Despite all the uncertainties that may surround you, despite all the confusion you may feel in trying to ascertain the Father's will or decide what courses of action to take, one of the constants that applies to all people in all places and situations is to make your next move a step of faith. Make your next response a commitment to put your confidence in God and in *whatever* He knows is ultimately best for you and will bring about the beauty He intends to create through your life, even from your suffering.

One of our favorite quotes from C. S. Lewis is a statement made by a fictitious senior demon named Screwtape to his nephew and protégé, Wormwood, in the classic book *The Screwtape Letters*. Screwtape's enemy, of course, is God. We thought of this line often throughout our journey with Jude and prayed that God would make us like the person mentioned here—someone the devil deems significantly troubling to his plans.

> Do not be deceived, Wormwood. Our cause is never more in
> danger than when a human, no longer desiring, but still intend-
> ing, to do our Enemy's will, looks round upon a universe from
> which every trace of Him seems to have vanished, and asks why
> he has been forsaken, and still obeys.[8]

The most powerful thing a Christ follower can do is obey God when nothing makes sense. Obedience always brings blessing, but not necessarily instant blessing. When we obey God but don't see the blessing right away, we need to keep stepping forward in obedience, knowing God is building up a greater eternal blessing that "far outweighs" all our troubles (2 Corinthians 4:17).

When the blessing is later, it's always greater. The problem is that we often stop taking steps of obedience when we don't see God come through immediately or as we expected Him to. When we stop taking steps of obedience in faith, we give the Enemy ground that God intended us to take.

It's easy to obey God when everything makes sense. But when you're walking through the valley God has told you to walk through and you can't see what He's doing, feel His presence, hear His voice, or taste His goodness because of the salt of your tears—and you obey anyway—that is the divine moment when you stop trusting your senses and start trusting your Savior.

When you obey God even when it doesn't make sense, you are making a huge faith statement to God, yourself, and others that you believe that the blessing may come later but it will be greater!

As Corrie ten Boom, the great Christ follower who survived a German concentration camp where her sister died under the cruel treatment of the guards, wrote, "When a train goes through a tunnel and it gets dark, you don't throw away your ticket and jump off. You sit still and trust the engineer."[9] You stay on the train because deep down you know it's going to its intended destination and the engineer is in control.

That's the way it is with God. Sometimes we don't understand what God is doing. We can't see what He is up to when we go through the dark tunnels of life. But in those dark tunnels, we just stay on the train, keep trusting, continue singing in faith—knowing that God's train is taking us toward His purpose for our lives and that no current problem can derail it.

Josh and Kelli didn't know what God was doing by letting Jude be so sick. The Lord did not always seem near, and there are still times when they can't feel His presence because the pain of loss seems overwhelming. But as best they can—imperfectly but with tenacity—they hold on to His promises with childlike faith.

KERRY'S STORY: THE RATTLING NOISE OF HOPE

After Jude went to be with the Lord, I turned to the passage in Ezekiel that had inspired Josh and Kelli to obey even when they didn't understand. As I read, my heart was filled with hope.

> I spoke this message, just as [God] told me. Suddenly as I spoke, there was a rattling noise all across the valley. The bones of each body came together and attached themselves as complete skeletons. (37:7, NLT)

Like Josh and Kelli, the prophet spoke in faith and left the results to the sovereign Lord, and suddenly there was a rattling noise as the dry bones were reattached. I love that! For Ezekiel, the rattling noise signified hope and life coming out of the valley of hopelessness and death. The noise continued to build into a rumble and roar of hope and life as the bones came alive.

I can hear that rattling noise of hope now as it builds and builds. It started with Josh and Kelli's obedience in speaking and singing life over

Jude, entrusting him to their sovereign Lord. It's the sound of hope and life coming out of the valley of hopelessness and death.

Jude is alive in heaven, but his life is reverberating hope here on this earth. And the rattling noise of life and hope continues to build.

A young man who'd been attending our church for a while took more than a passing interest in a video of Josh and Kelli that we showed at our Christmas Eve services shortly before Jude was born. Our son Ryan had flown to Cincinnati and shot the footage in a room at the Ronald McDonald House where they were staying, awaiting Jude's birth. Around forty thousand people saw that video at our services, but only one of them—this particular guy—had a brother in Cincinnati whose child had died from a very similar ailment at the same children's hospital where we'd been spending so much of our time.

Fast-forward, then, to January 8, the day Jude died. When we reported to the church that Jude had gone to be with the Lord, this young man suggested to his brother in Ohio that he watch the celebration service, which we'd arranged to broadcast online for friends and family living out of town. He did and was so touched by the faith and peace Josh expressed that he asked his brother who lived in Houston, "Do you think Josh would meet with me if I flew down there?"

On a Sunday morning a few weeks later, this man found Josh after the service and asked whether they could talk for a minute. Right there amid the hubbub of people filing out of the auditorium and heading to their Sunday activities, the faith that had kept Josh standing firm throughout months of crisis became the saving faith that brought healing to this grieving father who'd given up on ever seeing his world resume a steady orbit. People's lives were being changed because Josh and Kelli kept on choosing to walk in faith rather than run for cover. And the rattling noise of hope kept building.

It's just what faith does.

Not long before, on my way home from Cincinnati, I swear I could hear the echoing sound of dry bones coming to life. I was on a plane flying home with Jude's body for burial. I'd never realized it before, but I discovered through this process that it's actually a common thing on large flights for people to travel in the main cabin while a relative's body is being carried in the cargo hold.

In fact, during my trip, after one of the flight attendants stopped to tell me she was sorry for my loss, the man in the seat next to me said he'd done the same thing several months before. His mother had passed away, and he'd been responsible for transporting her body back to the town where her funeral was to take place. He said that it had been a terribly upsetting time for him and added that he still wasn't dealing with it well.

"You're a pastor, aren't you?" he asked.

"Yes."

"You just seem to have peace, even after what you've been through. I can see it."

"Well, it's been really hard," I said, "but, yes, God's really given us peace." And then I told him about Jesus.

Josh was blown away when I told him about the man I'd shared the gospel with, even as Jude's body was traveling underneath us on our way back to Houston. Jude *himself* wasn't there, of course. He was fully alive in heaven, and God was already using him to lead others to Christ.

Faith wins. Faith conquers. Faith is contagious when you choose to live in it, and it spreads to others even when it seems to be defeated by the presence of death, loss, and extreme adversity in our lives. God still uses us and our faith in Him "to spread the aroma of the knowledge of him everywhere" (2 Corinthians 2:14). "For everyone born of God overcomes the world. This is the victory that has overcome the world, even our faith" (1 John 5:4).

The rattling noise of hope is still building.

Josh is a gifted worship leader for Woodlands Worship, the worship ministry at our church, and he uses his songwriting and singing to minister to thousands of people every weekend.

One of Josh's most beautiful worship songs is called "Restore the Years," which he wrote soon after Jude went to heaven. He and Kelli continue to trust that God will restore the years and that they'll spend eternity with their son in heaven, and the dry bones of hopelessness keep rattling together and coming to life as Jude's life continues to influence so many.

Restore the Years

I am broken
Death is all around
From where I stand, Lord,
Looks like You've let me down
But I am nothing
And You are just
You make treasure out of dust

You know each hurt I hide
Every hope unspoken
By Your word I rise
And though I lived in fear
Throwing the days away
You restored my wasted years

I want answers
And I'm not alone
Still one thing I know
This world is not my home
How can we hope
For something more
Unless it's something
We're made for

Our rescue is coming
These dead bones will rise
The hope that was stolen
Is now raised to life[10]

Living the Lesson

When Nothing Makes Sense, Just Obey

Josh wrote these words in his song "Restore the Years":

I am broken

Death is all around

From where I stand, Lord,

Looks like You've let me down

Has there been a time in your life when it felt as if God let you down?

Read Hebrews 11:6. God is pleased when we obey in faith despite how we feel. Have you been living based on your feelings or based on your faith in Christ?

How have you seen God bring hope and peace in the middle of your pain? What lessons are you learning as you walk in faith with God?

If you wait to obey until you feel like it, you'll miss the blessing. What steps of obedience do you need to take today, whether you feel like it or not?

Read Isaiah 43:2. Write a prayer thanking God for His promise of provision and protection as you walk in faith today.

Everyone Needs Help, Including You

The way God designed our bodies is a model for understanding our lives together as a church: every part dependent on every other part, the parts we mention and the parts we don't, the parts we see and the parts we don't. If one part hurts, every other part is involved in the hurt, and in the healing. If one part flourishes, every other part enters into the exuberance.

—1 Corinthians 12:25–26, MSG

Until we can receive with an open heart, we are never really giving with an open heart. When we attach judgment to receiving help, we knowingly or unknowingly attach judgment to giving help.

—Brené Brown

When our oldest grandson, Ben, was two years old, he would cry when he couldn't do a task all by himself. Everyday frustrations, such as not being able to get his foot into his rain boot, would drive him to tears. Now that he's four, Ben has learned to accept the limitations of his ability and experience. He still prefers to be independent, but if he doesn't succeed at something after several tries, he calmly looks up and says, "I need a little bit of help."

If only we could be as honest about our needs as Ben. As adults, it's easy to see that being a toddler has distinct limitations. Ben is short and weighs just forty pounds. He can't read. Asking for help is a sign of wisdom because it means that he sees what's needed in a situation and knows he doesn't have what it takes.

So why don't we ask for help more often? And what about you? Are you facing a situation that, deep down, you know you're incapable of meeting in your own strength?

It's our reluctance to admit our weakness to other people that keeps us in need. God created us to work together, just like the individual cells and systems and limbs of the human body. You're *supposed* to need help! You're *designed* to need help!

The Bible collectively refers to Christ followers as *the body of Christ*. That's not just a phrase; it's a reality. An eyeball would be useless if it didn't have feet to carry it where it needed to see, a neck to turn it in the right direction, and a brain to interpret the images. Every part of a human body both *helps* the other systems and *needs help* from the other parts in order to function. Not one cell could exist on its own. So it is with the body of Christ. The only way to become fully functional is to embrace this give-and-take of life. Offering help and asking for it are both awkward. We need to get over that.

Earlier this year on a freezing January night, we wrapped up in blankets and sat in the backyard waiting for the Super Blood Wolf Moon eclipse. News stations had been talking about how spectacular this lunar eclipse would be, but we began to doubt them as our hands slowly froze onto the heavy binoculars.

Finally it began. A dark mouth began to take a bite out of the moon. As the bite got larger and larger, the sky got darker and darker until there was only a sliver of the once-giant moon. And then . . . Wow! The moon was entirely in the earth's shadow, and the change in lighting revealed the moon in its 3-D glory.

Of course, we know the moon is a sphere and not a flat circle, but now we could see it, as if God were holding a ball between His thumb and forefinger. We glanced at the two-dimensional stars dotting the sky and could scarcely begin to imagine the implications of what we were seeing. The sheer immensity! The billions upon trillions of galaxies *all* being held like this! The audacity of human brains attempting to assign a measurement to how big space is. As if God couldn't stretch His hands a little and widen it. Change it. Wipe it all away.

At first, the earth's shadow over the moon blocked our view of it. But when all went dark, we finally saw the truth of it more than ever before.

It was the same as we walked through Jude's journey with Josh and Kelli. As long as there was even a sliver of light, of hope, our view didn't change. Only when the world went black did we see clearly the explosive revealing of God's glory. He was the one who had been holding us all along.

We kept watching the lunar eclipse that night as the curtain of normalcy slowly dropped into place, but our knowledge of what was behind it remained. If your world has been slowly darkening and you feel as though your soul is being eclipsed, we want you to know this:

He is holding you.

You can't see it. You can't feel it.

But He's coming after you.

He will never let you go.

God is always holding us, and He often chooses to work through human hands.

BLESSED RECEIVING

We've been in full-time vocational ministry for over thirty years. If you're a Christ follower, you're in full-time ministry too! You might be a nurse, teacher, accountant, business manager, student, mom, sportswriter, salesperson, pilot, dad, secretary, or taxi driver. But if you're a Christian, those job titles just describe where and how you minister.

Being pastors means that, in general, being on the giving side of the equation feels normal because we're used to it. We feel competent when counseling a couple whose marriage is falling apart, dropping off a meal for someone in need, or sitting in the emergency room with a family as they wait for a loved one to come out of a risky surgery.

Most pastors encounter situations like this often enough that they're able to focus on other people's needs rather than their own insecurities. And we'll be honest: we like that side. Sign us up for the giving side every day of the week. We're comfortable there. Safe. It's not as if we never have problems—far from it! It's just that we don't like asking anyone for help.

Jude changed all that. The moment we found out about his kidney condition, we broke. The agony of what we might be facing was more than we could bear alone. Pain can be so isolating, but for the first time in our lives, our pain was greater than our ability to conceal it.

So we awkwardly did something we'd never done before. We stood in front of our church and told them how much we were hurting. How much we were hoping. How much we needed them. Our appeal wasn't polished or eloquent—just raw emotion from leaders they'd never seen cry.

What happened was profound. The people who had walked into our church as individuals responded as one body. They loved us. Hard. Like sheep hovering over a wounded shepherd, Woodlands Church showed more love and grace to our family than we could repay in a hundred lifetimes.

And here we need to admit something.

Before Jude, we'd never fully understood what it means to be part of the body of Christ. Sure, we knew the theology, but *hearing* a truth isn't the same thing as *experiencing* it. Now we can see it clearly.

We have learned the privilege of living in community. Together as the body of Christ, we celebrate the good times. We lean in and love hard in the difficult times. We challenge one another and ask hard questions. Why? So that we can help one another look more like Christ. None of us should *only* give or *only* take. We're here to bear witness to one another's lives.

The apostle Paul is a model of someone who "poured [himself] out like a drink offering" (2 Timothy 4:6) in order to care for the needs of others. There was no sacrifice he wouldn't make. There was no one else's shortage he wouldn't meet, no matter the cost to his own comfort or lifestyle. Yet as proactive and proficient as Paul proved himself to be in serving others, he was equally bold and unashamed in asking for and accepting help, being active on both sides of what he called "the matter of giving and receiving" (Philippians 4:15). Each role, he knew, is vital to our lives as Christians. We should be able to graciously receive just as we graciously give.

This really goes to the heart of the gospel. The main factor that keeps people from accepting Christ's death on the cross as forgiveness for their sins is that they don't think they need it. They're willing to work for it, of course, by doing good deeds. They just don't want to put themselves in the position of *receiving* it. But to accept Christ means coming to terms with the fact that you and I can do nothing to earn His love and favor. "It is the gift of God—not by works, so that no one can boast" (Ephesians 2:8–9).

Somewhere deep down underneath our resistance to receiving blessing from others is the same germ of pride and self-sufficiency that breeds resistance to the gospel. If we cannot seem to stomach the thought of others caring for us at times, our hearts are alerting us to a problem inside.

Do you detest the idea of ever feeling or appearing weak? That's a problem . . . because "God chose the weak things of the world to shame the strong" (1 Corinthians 1:27). He knows He can accomplish things through our weakness that would be impossible if we insisted on keeping up a facade of strength. He chose Jude—someone weaker and in more desperate need than most of us have ever been—to bless not only our lives but countless others as well. Four babies we know of have even been named after him! Have you ever made such an impact on someone's life that she named her *child* after you? We haven't either. But Jude lived his one day in a way that continues to bring endless glory to God. Isn't that the primary purpose of each of our lives, no matter how many years we live?

Our deficiencies, you see, create a vacuum for God to fill with His goodness. Our needs create opportunities for others to meet them. Jesus was right, of course, when He said, "It is more blessed to give than to receive" (Acts 20:35). But is it right for us to hog all the blessings? Shouldn't we also want to contribute to *others* being blessed, even if it means we're the weak ones benefiting from their strength?

The odd thing in all this is that we don't mind asking *God* for help. We don't mind showing *Him* the many sides of ourselves when we're struggling to endure, pleading with Him to meet our needs. But we often want Him to meet those needs privately. We'd like to keep our deficiencies just between God and us. Apparently, then, accepting help is not our real hang-up. Our problem is admitting to others that we need help. Our problem is saying, "I'm hurting here. I'm needy. I don't know what's coming. I'm feeling unsure and insecure." Our problem is embracing the humility required to let others be the ones He uses to meet us where we hurt.

So here's what we've learned: asking God for help and then not accepting it from human hands is a problem. We've learned not to let our need to be perceived as strong become a barrier to how God chooses to care for us. In this "matter of giving and receiving," we should be as devoted to one as to the other. Either side makes us part of what God is doing to bless our world.

A BLESSING ON BOTH SIDES

Late in the afternoon following Chris's interaction with the women in the hotel elevator, Josh and Kelli heard a knock at their door. Upon opening it, they saw what appeared to be the entire on-duty staff from the hotel where we were staying. As a group, they presented Josh and Kelli with a little plaque they'd made in memory of Jude. Can you believe that? It was their extremely thoughtful way of expressing sympathy for Josh and Kelli, along with their commitment to do whatever they could to serve and assist them while they were there. We'd never seen anything like it.

We continue to be astounded at that impromptu gift and at how Jude's one day of life could result in a little ceremony of sorts among strangers in a hotel doorway, just as it had led to all those "Do you need a hug?" moments also involving strangers.

And the more we dwell on them, the more we realize that the common denominator between all those encounters was our weakness. Our emptiness and lack of strength invited God's goodness to flow toward us. If we hadn't been desperately in need, none of these encounters would have happened. But because we were so depleted during those months, we received the loving touch of the Lord from the most unexpected sources, even as each person who cared for us received the blessing of being strong in our weakness.

Receiving is actually a win-win. A blessing on both sides. And the sooner we learn not to run from it, the sooner we'll be able to run into the comforting arms of our Father. We won't be afraid to be weak anymore; we'll be more afraid of not recognizing how utterly weak we are.

Giving is a win-win too. Whenever you see someone in need, get in the habit of immediately offering to help. With practice it will become easier to push aside feelings of awkwardness to offer a helping hand or hug just when someone needs it the most.

We know it's hard. We're all busy. We're running behind, and chances are we were running behind yesterday too. But fresh opportunities present themselves every day. And as the Bible says, these opportunities are not to be viewed as merely optional. We have an "obligation," Paul said, "to bear the weaknesses of those without strength, and not to please ourselves. Each one of us is to please his neighbor for his good, to build him up. For even Christ did not please himself" (Romans 15:1–3, CSB).

Because we are Christ followers, helping people who are hurting is our *job,* not our hobby. It's our main line, not our sideline. "Let no debt remain outstanding," Paul said two chapters earlier, "except the continuing debt to love one another, for whoever loves others has fulfilled the law" (13:8).

It's not a gift; it's a debt.

Caring for others is *our* responsibility.

So we should take inventory at regular intervals of what we've been given. Instead of leaving it to chance, we should look around and see how we can apply what we have to the needs around us. See a need; fill a need.

The Bible tells us that "God is able to bless you abundantly, so that in all things at all times, having all that you need, you will abound in every good work" (2 Corinthians 9:8).

In other words, He gives us what we need for giving. He "supplies seed to the sower" (verse 10). He increases our store of resources, enlarging us in areas where He chooses to do so. And He does this not to make us fat but to make us *fit* for being a blessing, to give us stashes of abundance that we can use to fill those spaces where others are depleted. Paul continued, "You will be enriched in every way so that you can be generous on every occasion" (verse 11).

Now, maybe you don't feel as though you have anything extra. But if God promised He would enrich you "in every way so that you can be generous on every occasion," there must be some selective blindness going on if you see nothing of value in your supply chain. Take inventory of your resources:

- Are you sure you've made good use of all the time you've been given?
- Is there any money left over after wisely covering your needs and savings?
- Does your pantry contain any nonperishables that you'll probably never open?
- Do you have any useful items in your home that you haven't touched in years?
- Have you been eating better and exercising a little and therefore have more energy?
- Did God show you in His Word today a strong, encouraging promise?
- Are you in one of those periods of life when everybody's getting along?

What we're talking about here doesn't even get close to true sacrifice. It simply requires opening your mind to what you have and considering how you might share it.

If God has given you an abundance of something, more than you need for yourself—time, money, food, possessions, energy, insight, joy, whatever—then He probably means for it to go to somebody else. He provided it not only for *you* to experience good from it but also for you to be the conduit through which He blesses someone else.

Listen, this represents a real change in thinking for most of us. We're not accustomed to passing along our excess to others. We're trained by economics, not to mention motivated by greed and self-protection, to count the presence of extra in our lives as merely our good fortune. We're inclined toward either consuming it or stockpiling it.

What we've learned from our grandson who lived only a single day is that we don't have the luxury of hanging on to things until tomorrow, when other people could benefit from them today.

If we see excess in our lives anywhere, the only real question we ought to be asking is this: How and with whom are we supposed to share it?

So, let's see . . . what does obedience look like for you today?

The answer is found by seeing the excess you possess and then noticing who might need it most.

Open Your Heart; Open Your Home

After Jude went to heaven, Josh and Kelli realized they had a surplus of love to share and an unused bedroom, which would have been Jude's room, in their little home.

They clung to Jude's verses, choosing to believe that "love [was] on the way," and decided to become certified foster parents.

> I, Jude, am a slave to Jesus Christ . . . writing to those loved by
> God the Father, called and kept safe by Jesus Christ. Relax,

everything's going to be all right; rest, everything's coming together; open your hearts, love is on the way! (Jude 1:1–2, MSG)

Their decision was based not on feelings but on a very practical spiritual principle: we have a surplus, which means someone else must have a need. Now, how can we find that person?

As they worked through this process, Josh and Kelli shared with us about a little-known aspect of the foster parent program called respite care. It's designed to create a pool of on-call people who can temporarily house one or more children, simply as a way of giving foster parents a short break—maybe to get away for a weekend, handle some personal business, or just go out for a date night. It's not hard to imagine the need for foster parents to recharge now and then.

But here's the deal. Yes, it's a critical need for foster parents. But, at least in our city, it turns out it's not a service that's readily available. Do you know why? Because almost no one is certified and prepared to do it.

Legal requirements demand that people be authorized by the state before they can supervise foster children in their home, even for the evening. A respite caregiver must pass a background check, receive CPR instruction, go through the training and questionnaire process, and be certified.

We learned from the Child Protective Services staff in our county, which is home to more than half a million residents, that there are only a handful of people certified to provide respite care to foster parents. Doesn't add up to a lot of either care or respite. In fact, with statistics like that, we'd say even the respite care workers are in dire need of respite care. That's an astounding, gaping need in our midst. And we had been totally unaware of it.

So we took it upon ourselves to change that. During our church services one weekend, we made an appeal to the congregation, asking them to consider undergoing the process to become certified as a respite care individual or family. We simply presented the need and encouraged people to pray about it, and we provided information for those who wanted to learn more.

Now, obviously not everybody has the time to commit to something like this. Nor has God given every person a heart for reaching out in this way. And that's fine. There are a thousand other ways to give out of your surplus. But let's just say, for example, that this was a need in your community (it's quite likely it is). Is it possible you'd have the bandwidth to do it? Even just occasionally? Do you have any abilities or resources in abundance that you could divert in this direction? Could you provide foster parents with a rest so they could be better with their families and jobs?

Foster parenting or foster family support may not be your thing, but we know there's *something*. There's a regular commitment you could make, just as there are random as-you-go opportunities that crop up every day. And maybe you've already come up with an idea, even as you've been reading, of a particular resource you could bring out of your abundance and put toward others' needs. Think of it as something to get excited about. Think of it as giving Christ active claim over everything He's given you. Think of it as seeing your excess multiplied even further.

Think of it, friend, as a responsibility.

That weekend at church, more than 350 people volunteered to help our community of foster parents—a *hundred times* more than there had been before. And all it took was one couple, spurred on by what God had given them in abundance through their one little boy.

What has He given to *you*? What do you have that someone else is longing for?

What a difference it could make.

You could be the love that is on the way for someone today. But first you have to open your heart to receive love. As you learn to open your heart, you'll surrender your pride and admit that not only do you need God's help but you need it through human hands. That's when you'll discover the love that was right there all along, waiting for you.

Living the Lesson

Everyone Needs Help, Including You

Are you more comfortable receiving help or giving it? Why do you think that is?

What has prevented you from asking for help in the past? How do you think this has affected you and those you love?

Read 1 Corinthians 12:25–26 (MSG). Why do you think it's so important to be connected to the body of Christ? How have you seen the body of Christ building one another up?

Describe a situation that is beyond your ability to fix or that you're struggling to cope with. Ask God to show you how you can be more open to receiving help from other people.

God blesses us so we can be a blessing to others. Ask God to give you opportunities to be a better receiver and a better giver. Watch with expectation to see what happens and record it in your miracle book.

Fear and Faith Can't Occupy the Same Space

When we heard that, we and everyone there that day begged Paul not to be stubborn and persist in going to Jerusalem. But Paul wouldn't budge: "Why all this hysteria? Why do you insist on making a scene and making it even harder for me? You're looking at this backward. The issue in Jerusalem is not what they do to me, whether arrest or murder, but what the Master Jesus does through my obedience. Can't you see that?"

—Acts 21:12–13, MSG

Faith means believing what you don't yet see, and the reward of this faith is to see what you believe.

—Saint Augustine

K elli's contractions had started up again. We'd hoped her pregnancy could hold out a while longer. But there was no way of stopping labor anymore.

The best-case scenarios for Jude were dependent on maintaining a normal-length gestation. Time was his friend. Every day he could remain inside the warmth and nourishment of his mother's body raised his chances of survival by a click or two. But now, with Kelli at roughly thirty weeks—not quite seven months—his entrance into the world appeared imminent. Jude was coming—premature—the next day.

So you could feel the tension mounting in the room that night, along with Kelli's discomfort. She'd worked with such tenacity both to stave off her labor and now to let it happen.

At some point in the evening, when we felt sure that she and Josh were amply supplied with everything they needed, we realized the best thing we could do would be to leave them to themselves so they could rest and just be together. This was their moment to share in their own way, as their own little family.

Whatever hours of sleep any of us could get that night would translate into stamina for what was certain to be a long day tomorrow, no matter how things ended up going with Jude. We left the hospital, hoping we'd be standing there within twenty-four hours, wide awake, praying, willing our little grandson through his first day of life on his way to many, many more.

CHRIS'S STORY: IN THE PAW OF A LION

Upon arriving back at the hotel, I almost instantly crashed into bed. I doubted I'd be able to stay asleep for long, but it was deep while it lasted . . . deep enough for my subconscious to begin an intensely vivid dream.

Scientists claim we dream every night, and I don't know about you, but I don't often remember my dreams clearly. This particular dream, though, was stunning. I can still remember every detail, especially one really strong image from it.

Somehow I was being held in the paw of a lion—which obviously should have made this dream more of a nightmare. Instead, I was keenly aware of an all-encompassing peace, the utter confidence and comfort of being completely protected from harm and untouchable. It was beautiful. Soothing. Perfectly calm. It felt like . . . like I was all right. Like *all* was *right*.

Amazingly, this peaceful feeling held for several long moments, even as I awakened in the still-dark hours of the morning. I lay there silently, overwhelmed by an inner prompting to worship . . . because, yes, I was indeed held in the paw of a lion—the Lion of Judah. Josh and Kelli—along with Jude—were also clasped securely in the paw of the Lion. Not as prey, in which case a lion's paw would be the most terrifying place you could be, but as the Lion's cubs, which made the Lion's paw the safest, most comforting place of all.

This just illustrates how your outlook influences everything in your life. Your attitude depends on what you're *seeing*—whether you're looking at life only with your actual eyes and through your habitual patterns of thinking or you're seeing something more . . . seeing what is *unseen.*

Because there is so much to see in that which is unseen.

Paul said, "Our struggle is not against flesh and blood, but against the rulers, against the authorities, against the powers of this dark world and against the spiritual forces of evil in the heavenly realms" (Ephesians 6:12). Did you realize that? We look at our problems and can describe each one of them, down to the most intricate detail. Turns out, though, we don't know even the half of it. Our problems, as bad as they may be, are actually much, much worse than we thought. We know only the part we *see.* We wouldn't believe the *un*seen.

Yet if you pull that biblical viewfinder closer, you'll discover something else. Despite all the spiritual opposition you are up against daily, God has given you everything you need to "be strong in the Lord and in his mighty power." He enables you to put on His "full armor . . . so that when the day of evil comes, you may be able to stand your ground, and after you have done everything, to stand" (verses 10, 13).

None of these weapons are visible: "the belt of truth," "the breastplate of righteousness," "the shield of faith," and so on (verses 14, 16). But they're real. As a child of God, you have access to them for defense against the Enemy. Although you may have doubts at times, you can trust God to be as strong for you as His armor advertises. He will use this unseen equipment to remind you of your identity in Him, to accomplish your victory in Him, and to solidify your absolute certainty that "the one who is in you is greater than the one who is in the world" (1 John 4:4).

Now, maybe you wouldn't know it to look at you. You wouldn't know it to look at me. But if you and I were purposefully looking beyond the visible on a daily basis, we could walk in this spirit of confidence no matter how horrible our circumstances. We could wake up each morning—like I did in the hotel room the day Jude was born—recognizing we're safe within the palm of His hand, even if everything is making us feel as though we're about to be clawed to death.

So I wasn't surprised God gave me this kind of dream on that kind of night . . . because throughout our time in Cincinnati, He'd been giving me little opportunities to recognize His nearness and reliability. To encourage me. To steady me. To help me see the unseen.

You may not have chosen many of the circumstances that you face today, but you *do* get to choose what to focus on. You get to decide whether to direct your attention to what your five senses are telling you or to focus on what God tells you in His Word and in your heart. Choose wisely: whatever you focus on will expand. Fear will give birth to more fear, and faith will grow into more faith.

Paul, an Example of Fortitude

My favorite book in the Bible is Philippians. The first time I read it, I was fourteen years old and had recently heard the gospel for the first time. I knew I wanted to know Jesus and serve Him, but I had no idea how to go about it. I started reading the Bible and quickly became confused by all the unfamiliar names and phrases, but when I got to Philippians, I felt as if I'd found the prize in a scavenger hunt. Aha! So *this* is how you do it! This is how to live like Jesus!

To understand Philippians, you have to understand Paul, the man who wrote it. As a young man from Tarsus, Paul (also known as Saul) had everything going for him. He was a Greek-speaking Jew and a Roman citizen during a time when Rome was the world's superpower. He was an ultrareligious Jew who came from a well-respected family and meticulously followed all the rules. He was well educated and skilled at tent making, which allowed him to find work anywhere. But he'd chosen to use his privileged position to mercilessly torment and abuse Jewish converts to Christianity (see Galatians 1:13–14; Philippians 3:6).[11]

But one day as he was traveling to a town called Damascus, Jesus appeared to Paul in a vision and confronted him about his actions. After Paul experienced three days of blindness, God restored his physical eyesight and also gave him the ability to see spiritual things clearly (see Acts 9:1–19).

Paul's immediate and lifelong reaction was to proclaim that Jesus is the Son of God. For the rest of his days, he used every ounce of his experiences—both positive and shameful—to add credence to his claims about Jesus. Paul explained in his own words why he didn't shy away from any part of his life story: "I have become all things to all people so that by all possible means I might save some. I do all this for the sake of the gospel, that I may share in its blessings" (1 Corinthians 9:22–23).

I think it's safe to say that Paul endured more tough times than most of us ever will. You think you've had a hard life? In his second letter to the Corinthian church, he listed some of the challenges he'd faced. Paul

- was flogged by Jews five times with thirty-nine lashes
- was beaten by Roman rods three times

- was pummeled with rocks
- was shipwrecked three times
- was adrift on the open sea for a night and a day
- traveled hard year in and year out
- forded rivers
- fought off robbers
- struggled with friends and enemies
- endured risky conditions in the city, in the wilderness, and during storms at sea
- was betrayed by people he thought were dear friends
- served hard labor
- was often lonely, sleepless, hungry, and freezing cold
- felt the constant weight of responsibility for supporting, training, and encouraging all the churches
- experienced deep desperation[12]

And this list was written just partway through his ministry! Paul's words take on new meaning when we know what he went through. As he wrote the book of Philippians, he was between a rock and a hard place once again—this time shackled in a Roman jail cell. I've been inside the cave-like prison in Rome where Paul most likely sat as he penned this letter. Two thousand years later, it's still incredibly depressing, even without the foul smell.

Paul wrote the short four-chapter letter to the Philippians under these conditions. You'd expect it to be overflowing with complaints. Bitterness. Fear. But no, against every set of odds in the universe, Paul was bursting with *joy*.

His friends had no doubt heard he was chained up in prison, and he wanted to be sure they understood the plain truth about his situation.

I want you to know, brothers and sisters, that what has happened to me has actually served to advance the gospel. As a result, it has become clear throughout the whole palace guard and to everyone else that I am in chains for Christ. And because of my chains, most of the brothers and sisters have become confident in the Lord and dare all the more to proclaim the gospel without fear.

It is true that some preach Christ out of envy and rivalry, but others out of goodwill. The latter do so out of love, knowing that I am put here for the defense of the gospel. The former preach Christ out of selfish ambition, not sincerely, supposing that they can stir up trouble for me while I am in chains. But what does it matter? The important thing is that in every way, whether from false motives or true, Christ is preached. And because of this I rejoice.

Yes, and I will continue to rejoice. (1:12–18)

Paul explained that they were looking at his chains all wrong! The *only* goal of his life, he reminded them, was to advance the gospel. It wasn't just his top priority; it was the *only* one. And as a direct result of his imprisonment, the gospel was being heard by more people. Paul said in effect, "My chains are a huge win! My pain and limitations are so valuable because they're enabling me to achieve my goal."

When I first read this, I was blown away by Paul's perspective. I still am, even as I write this. Let me be honest: while it's easy to recognize the upside of other people's limitations, I am nearly incapable of seeing the value of my own. Just like you and me, Paul had made plans. His missionary journeys and international church visits had to have involved a huge number of details. But Paul never lost sight of the overriding goal of his life. Instead of complaining about how his current situation prevented him from continuing with his plans to tell people about Jesus, he saw his imprisonment as a divine appointment. Paul knew what he was to do—share Christ's story. He left it to God to decide to whom, where, when, and how that would unfold. He trusted that God had him right where He wanted him.

Have you ever stopped to consider how many decisions in your life are dictated by fear? Fear of failure. Fear of shame. Fear of hurt. We try to manage our lives in such a way that we will avoid fresh hurt. The problem is that no matter how hard we try to avoid it, pain finds us. I appreciate that Jesus was straightforward about this, acknowledging, "In this world you will have trouble. But take heart! I have overcome the world" (John 16:33).

Paul's jail sentence was a great thing for the prison guards because they got to hear all about Jesus. And his imprisonment is a great thing for you and me too! If Philippians had been written by a guy who was relaxing on a Mediterranean beach, it wouldn't mean much to me. I'd think, *Well, of* course *you're happy. I would be too if I were in your sandals! But I have real problems going on in my life right now. Bills to pay, sick kids to care for, struggles to work out in my relationships . . . stuff you clearly don't understand.* And I'd close the book.

Seeing a clear picture of what Paul endured gives his testimony the weight of truth. This guy simply wouldn't have been in prison if he wasn't positive that the one who stopped him on the road to Damascus was the Son of the living God. His absolute faith and confidence in this Jesus had jettisoned every scrap of fear from his mind.

FEAR NOT

Fear and faith can't occupy the same space. If one decreases, the other can increase, but just like a full bottle of oil and vinegar, you have to have less of one in order to add more of the other. We tend to think that we can measure our value by adding up the recordable facts of our lives. That we are only as good as our spreadsheet balances, grades, titles, and degrees. The truth, of course, is that these are just meaningless facts that will become increasingly worthless as time passes. On the other hand, the *unseen* aspects of our lives—such as our character and the condition of our hearts—have eternal implications of such magnitude we can scarcely grasp it.

The facts of our lives, the measurable parts that can be recorded, have value only inasmuch as they provide opportunities to work out our faith. We are all imperfect and prone to sin. How are we going to go from full of sin to full of faith unless we have opportunities to practice? Seen in this way, life becomes a series of practice tests. And just like a practice test for a college entrance exam or professional certification, our score is an accurate indicator of our abilities or, in this case, our hearts.

We'd like to think that if we do poorly on a practice test, our performance can be explained away with a valid excuse. Maybe we didn't really try our hardest. Or we were tired, stressed, hungry, or sick, so our score shouldn't count.

Ultimately, though, life reveals that the little things *are* the big things. The things that are unseen—our thoughts, motivations, character, and hearts—are what are being tested. Our spiritual lives as believers become a lifelong process of reconciling what we perceive with our senses with what Scripture tells us is true.

Here's our truth: We ache for Jude. We desperately want him here, in our arms. We believe that we will be together again someday, but some days this temporary separation feels unbearable.

And this is also our truth: this pain that feels crushing and permanent will someday be replaced with something so glorious that we'll see the pain as light and momentary. We don't understand why Jude's story was written this way, and we don't expect to in this lifetime. But if these chains serve to advance the gospel, what does it matter? We are counting on Jesus to hold us up one day at a time. We eagerly expect Him to fill us with courage so that our lives will be used to elevate Christ.

You see, in the end our circumstances weren't changed. We were.

Living the Lesson

Fear and Faith Can't Occupy the Same Space

You can't help it when fear invades your life, but you do have a choice about how you respond to it. You can choose to focus on the fear and give in to it, or you can choose to turn toward God in faith. In what specific ways can you choose to focus on faith instead of fear in your current circumstances?

Read Ephesians 6:10–18. Which piece of armor or weapon do you need most today? Spend a few minutes in prayer, asking God to help you stand firm in His strength today.

Can you think of a time when you asked God to change your situation but instead He used the situation to change you?

How many of your decisions have been based on fear? Whether it's the fear of failure, fear of rejection, or fear of the future, we all tend to let fear drive our lives. What is your greatest fear?

Today, choose to step out in faith in spite of your fears. Write a prayer asking God to help you focus on His greatness as you release your fear into His overwhelming love.

If You're Still Breathing, It's a Good Day

Not that I was ever in need, for I have learned how to be content with whatever I have. I know how to live on almost nothing or with everything. I have learned the secret of living in every situation, whether it is with a full stomach or empty, with plenty or little. For I can do everything through Christ, who gives me strength.

—Philippians 4:11–13, NLT

It isn't what you have or who you are or where you are or what you are doing that makes you happy or unhappy. It is what you think about it.

—Dale Carnegie

Throughout our time in Cincinnati, knowing the situation Jude was in, we often held up a litmus test to one another: "Are everyone's kidneys working today? Yes? Okay, good. Then it's a good day." As long as our kidneys were operational, we could keep going. Instead of holding our day up against the good things others possessed that we didn't, we chose to focus on the good things we had that some folks would love to claim as their own.

We had many other yardsticks at our disposal, of course, that we could've used for assessing the faithfulness of the Lord. But to us, because of Jude's story, functioning kidneys were not a given. They were the whole reason we were there. And the fact that ours were working in the background every day was a blessing we did not want to overlook.

It didn't make our hard thing any easier, checking on the status of one another's kidneys. But it did help keep our hard thing in perspective. And changing our perspective is a big part of living with a one-day mindset.

Jude was teaching us an important lesson about gratitude. Gratitude unclouds your vision so you are able to clearly recognize God's blessings and truly appreciate them. What we're saying is, don't miss what you have because of what you don't! We often fail to see the greatest blessings in our lives and appreciate them because we're focused on what we don't have. We often look past the blessings right in front of us as we search for that future blessing that will solve all our problems. Could it be that the miracle you're looking for is right under your nose? You may be looking past it because you haven't allowed gratitude to clear up your blurry vision.

The Bible tells us that is exactly what happened to the people in Christ's day: "He was in the world, and the world was created through him, and yet the world did not recognize him" (John 1:10, CSB). The God of the universe was walking among them, and they didn't realize it. They were looking for the miracle of the Messiah in the future, and they missed the miracle in the present. Jesus Christ Himself right in their presence!

If you fail to see the miracle in today, you'll never recognize the miracle in tomorrow.

Just imagine that we were standing in front of a blank white wall and we took out a red marker and made a small dot. Then we stopped and asked you to look at the wall and tell us what you saw. If you're like most people, you would simply reply, "I see a small red dot." Of course, you'd be right. The problem is that most of us would fail to see that 99 percent of what we were looking at was white!

Of course, it's just human nature to focus on what stands out and forget about the rest. We all tend to zero in on the red dot of difficulties and fail to notice the vast canvas of God's goodness in our lives.

ENOUGH IS ENOUGH

Do you feel as though you're never enough? In large part, that's because we've been told what our lives should look like and we've bought into the lie without even questioning the absurdity of it. The big lie we've believed that has us questioning our value and our sanity is "You can have it all, right now!"

Let us explain. We are told that we should have exciting careers and be moving up the ladder in fulfilling jobs that use all our passions and giftings. At the same time, we should have storybook romances where we go on long walks with our beloved and have deep conversations for hours each day; we should constantly travel to exotic places and experience other cultures to broaden our horizons; we should cook gourmet meals that are healthy, colorful, and eaten at fabulously decorated tables sprinkled with a few seasonal items . . . in houses that are tidy and charming yet sophisticated; we should be focused on being physically fit and go to the gym regularly; we should get plenty of sleep so we can be mentally alert; we should grow intellectually by keeping up with our book clubs; we should learn a second or third language and stay up to speed on current world events to be responsible citizens; and we should plan creative activities for our kids that reduce screen time and help build their character along with developing their intellect.

Oh, and we need to make sure we look sexy, smart, and put together while we do it!

We have been told that we should be and have all this and more—and because we're not and we don't, we feel inadequate. We don't appreciate what we have because we're so focused on what we don't have.

Here's the truth that will set you free: you can have it all, but not all at the same time.

Until we get that through our heads and into our hearts, we will always feel as though we are not enough.

God never designed you to do it all at the same time. Ecclesiastes 3:1 says, "To everything there is a season, a time for every purpose under heaven" (NKJV).

God designed us to go through different seasons of life. His creation operates in cycles and seasons. In the summer a tree is filled with green leaves that provide shade. In the fall the same tree is filled with beautiful leaves of orange or yellow or red. In the winter after the leaves have fallen, there is a stark beauty in the dark branches against the white snow, and in the spring there are buds and new life. These are all good seasons, but they don't happen at the same time. God designed our lives to go through seasons too. Start thanking God for the blessings He is providing in the season you're currently in.

How do we practice gratitude for our current season? Well, let's do what Jude taught us to do. Break the season down into single days. One day at a time. The psalmist tells us, "This is the day the LORD has made; we will rejoice and be glad in it" (118:24, NKJV).

Such a small and simple yet profound verse. This is the day. *Today.* This one day is the day God made for you and for us, and we can rejoice and be glad in it and be grateful for it. Gratitude is always a choice.

GRATEFUL FOR GRIEF

The tears of grief can easily wash away the treasure of gratitude. When you're just trying to make it through the day, it's hard to see the blessings. In the middle of grieving, it's important to realize that grieving itself is a blessing from God.

Jesus said in Matthew 5:4, "Blessed are those who mourn, for they will be comforted." Jesus was saying that not only is it okay to grieve, cry, and feel deep sadness, but it's also a blessed gift from God. Grieving is the process God uses in our lives to bring comfort and healing. If we run from our grief or stuff it down or hide from it, we deny ourselves our only hope, the comfort of the God who understands grief.

In our culture we have an aversion to grief. We like to skip over grief or hurry up the process because we think it's bad to feel sad. Sadness is not bad. It was created by God to help us in the healing process. If you short-circuit the grieving process by rushing through it or thinking God wants you to act happy, the grief will eventually explode onto the scene of your life, usually in devastating and destructive behaviors.

David, the writer of most of the psalms, knew how to grieve. There are 150 psalms total, and fifty of them include complaints to God. They are psalms of lament in which David poured out his hurt, confusion, and anger to God. He said things like "God, what are You doing? This makes no sense to me!" and "God, I don't understand. I'm so angry and confused!" Here are a few verses that highlight David's emotional appeals:

Can't you see I'm black-and-blue,
>   beat up badly in bones and soul?
GOD, how long will it take
>   for you to let up? (6:2–3, MSG)

Long enough, GOD—
>   you've ignored me long enough. (13:1, MSG)

God, God . . . my God!
>   Why did you dump me
>   miles from nowhere? (22:1, MSG)

David always poured out his grief to God. But he always came back to trust and gratitude, saying something like "I don't see it right now, but I know You'll see me through. I know You are God, and even though I don't see it now, I know deep down that You're going to fulfill Your promise to me." These verses convey his unwavering trust:

If your heart is broken, you'll find GOD right there;
if you're kicked in the gut, he'll help you catch your breath.
    (34:18, MSG)

At dusk, dawn, and noon I sigh
    deep sighs—he hears, he rescues. (55:17, MSG)

GOD keeps an eye on his friends,
his ears pick up every moan and groan. . . .
Is anyone crying for help? GOD is listening,
ready to rescue you. (34:15, 17, MSG)

When we admit our pain to God and stop trying to deny our grief, we are choosing to be grateful for the gift of grieving and can then experience God's healing. Healing is found not only in happiness but also in sadness. His healing will sustain you through the pain until you can once again see the blessings of God all around you.

GRATITUDE BRINGS AWARENESS

Every parent knows that watching your child endure pain is exponentially more difficult than enduring it yourself. Since we were surrounded by parents walking through the unimaginable, we found that even on the darkest days, there was so much to be grateful for.

Thank You, Lord, that Jude isn't in pain.

Thank You, Lord, that Jude is strong and kicking.

This naturally led to specific prayers for the kids and parents we'd met that day. Prayer began to come as naturally to us as breathing.

Lord, we need You this minute.

Oh, thank You—You did it again, God.

Father, would You help that family we just met?

Oh yes, God. We will reach out to that person right now!

Every day we could draw a direct line tracing the trail of our prayers from thankfulness to provision. The path started in the morning with gratitude for what we had—even if it was no more than a heartbeat—and ended with God still holding us up at the end of the day. Living that way will leave you with a deep awareness of God's work in and around you. It's a journey you'll never regret.

CHRIS'S STORY: NOW AND WHEN

Several years ago I had the opportunity to visit the great Colosseum in Rome. What a marvel! Everything about it is impressive, from its massive size to its perfectly proportioned arches. It seems I couldn't go more than a few steps without discovering something I just *had* to document with a picture.

Before leaving for the day, I bought an interesting little souvenir book containing modern-day photographs of important historic sites in Rome, including the Colosseum. What makes the book intriguing is that each picture includes a clear plastic overlay with an artist's rendering of what the place looked like in its heyday. One moment you're looking at ancient ruins, and then with a turn of the page, the crumbling walls are tall and erect, the faded paint has been transformed into gleaming Technicolor, and empty spaces are filled in with wooden doors and paths. You see each site as a whole. As it was meant to be. As it *should* be.

Just like that, my perspective changed.

I looked back up at the Colosseum. What I'd thought was wondrous just moments before suddenly seemed shabby and decrepit. Focusing on the perfect image had left me dissatisfied with the real one.

I didn't know at the time that God would use that experience many years later during our journey with Jude. Our time in Cincinnati included a near-constant succession of doctor appointments, scans, and heart-stopping trips to the emergency room. Kelli's eyes would fill with tears as she bravely endured yet another painful procedure in behalf of her son, and I'd think, *It's not supposed to be this way!* Always before me, superimposed on what I *had* was what I *wanted*. But comparing our current circumstances with our dreamed-up version of perfection is dangerous.

If we let this become a habit, we'll end up missing out on the very best parts of our lives. You see, Jude was—and is—a perfect boy. True, his kidneys weren't working and his lungs were underdeveloped, but that didn't stop us from marveling at what we *did* have.

We marveled at all his perfection! Those peach-soft round cheeks. That perfect nose and dark blond hair. His tiny fingernails, like a row of little pink seashells. And, most arresting of all, his calm blue-eyed gaze.

Yes, the problems were still there. But can't you see all that was right? Looked at from a medical standpoint, his kidneys and lungs were in ruins. The same thing can be said of many people near the end of their lives. Someday it might be true of you and me.

It doesn't really matter, though, does it? After all, our lives aren't defined by what bodily system ultimately fails us. Our lives are defined by the people we touch. We live to tell the story of the Savior. And by that standard, Jude was richer than many people who live for eighty years.

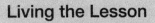

Living the Lesson

If You're Still Breathing, It's a Good Day

What would it look like to view your life with eyes of gratitude? List at least five blessings in your life right now and then express your thanks to God.

Read Philippians 4:11–13 (NLT). Paul tells us that he's learned the secret of contentment. Do you struggle with being content? Are you missing the blessing of what you have because you're focused on what you don't have?

Is there an area in your life where you have avoided feeling grief or sadness? Write down what you feel and don't hold back. Remember, these feelings were created by God to help you heal.

Do you ever find yourself comparing your current circumstances with what you thought your life would be like? How has this held you back or kept you from appreciating what you have?

Ask God to help you live with a heart of gratitude, appreciating the amazing gift of today. Write down three small changes you could make or habits you could develop to help keep your focus on your blessings.

You Don't Have to Pray.
You Get to Pray.

Do not be anxious about anything, but in every situation, by prayer and petition, with thanksgiving, present your requests to God. And the peace of God, which transcends all understanding, will guard your hearts and your minds in Christ Jesus.

—PHILIPPIANS 4:6–7

I have been driven many times upon my knees by the overwhelming conviction that I had nowhere else to go. My own wisdom and that of all about me seemed insufficient for that day.

—ABRAHAM LINCOLN

t's easy to think of daily prayer and Bible reading as a chore, as an unwanted assignment. Sometimes our tendency is to feel as if those few moments of private devotion are the anomaly, as if the real world is what's going on after we put away our Bibles. It often feels as though we're too busy today to stop and take time to pray.

But the opposite is actually true. Opening the Scriptures and our hearts to God in prayer each morning is like opening the window on an unseen world. It's like putting on reading glasses that bring everything into clearer focus, enabling us to view the rest of our day through a different lens, seeing it with a truer, more eternal perspective. Where beforehand we had to strain to see Him, now we can see things that are actually even closer than our problems. The *unseen* is what we're looking for now. When we take time to stop and realign our thoughts with God's perspective, we're ready to head into the day freshly attuned and alert, inviting Him to show us where He can use us today.

God loves it when we prioritize the unseen above our natural craving for the tangible. He doesn't require us to perform for Him in order to receive His acceptance; He rewards our daily prayer, our daily faith, our daily "confidence in what we hope for and assurance about what we do not see" (Hebrews 11:1). When we go into each day—even our hardest days—on the lookout for what's unseen, we never know what He will show us.

Prayer, of course, is an essential element in keeping our spiritual eyes peeled for what our physical eyes miss. That's why Jesus, in teaching His disciples how to pray, contrasted genuine prayer with the kind practiced by many of the religious professionals of His day, who saw prayer primarily as a performance.

Jesus said these people's motivation in prayer was "to be seen by others" (Matthew 6:5). They saw prayer selfishly as a means to an end, focusing on what it could do for them. But prayer is not just an outward exercise. It's an experience with the unseen God. Jesus said, "When you pray, go into your room, close the door and pray to your Father, who is unseen. Then your Father, who sees what is done in secret, will reward you" (verse 6).

Unseen? Yes, that's the way our physical eyes encounter God in prayer, isn't it? No visible proof that He is really here. No sign that He is actively listening. No logical reason for thinking these words of ours are doing anything of consequence, except maybe keeping us from a half-dozen other activities that we might deem to be more productive uses of our time.

Yet Jesus promises a reward when we spend time talking to Him: the reward of His presence. The reward of being squarely in His will, of pleasing Him simply by admitting we need Him. The reward of being drawn closer to His side, of our hearts growing more tender so He can more easily communicate to us through His Word and His Spirit . . . so the unseen God can show us things we've never seen before.

Do we really want to miss a single day of that?

Kerry's Story: Knocked Down, Raised Up

If we're honest, we usually pray because we're in a desperate situation, not because we are so aware that it's a divine privilege. I don't know about you, but I've found that my problems turn me to prayer.

I think that's a huge reason God wants us to be thankful in the middle of the trials of life. Without problems, I would never discover the treasure of pouring out my heart to God and watching Him work powerfully in my life.

In 2 Corinthians 12:7, Paul tells us there was a time when the Enemy tried to finish him off: "Satan's angel did his best to get me down; what he in fact did was push me to my knees" (MSG). Paul was saying that Satan's attacks were an attempt to knock him out of the game, but Satan's plan backfired. Instead of keeping Paul from his purpose, it knocked Paul to his knees, where he found more of God's power.

I have to admit that if I hadn't experienced a struggle with anxiety and depression, I wouldn't be nearly as close to God as I am today. The Enemy tried to use anxiety attacks to knock me away from my purpose, but they just knocked me to my knees and taught me how to lean on God more and humbly admit I need others as well.

I also know the Enemy has tried to use the pain we're experiencing from missing Jude to keep us from fulfilling our purpose, but it's had the opposite effect. The pain has moved us to prayer, and prayer has moved us into God's purpose more than ever. One day at a time, we choose to admit our pain and resist the urge to avoid or dismiss our grief. Instead, we run into God's arms and discover what we were made for—a love relationship with our Creator.

A Letter to God

The Bible has so many practical examples of how leaders dealt with their problems. One of my favorites is a guy named Hezekiah. When his story picks up in 2 Kings 18, the Assyrians had already attacked the northern kingdom of Israel several years earlier and taken them into captivity. Before long they'd turned their greedy eyes on the southern kingdom as well, which was under the rule of King Hezekiah.

Unlike most of the kings who followed in David's royal line, Hezekiah was a good leader, a godly man. Still, the threat of disaster from Assyria's king, Sennacherib, was terrifying. (Sennacherib's name alone sounds like a punch in the stomach.)

Hezekiah tried bargaining with him, offering to pay whatever price it would take for him to leave Judah in peace. Sennacherib's price was an insane amount of silver and gold. Wanting to protect his people, Hezekiah complied, even though it meant stripping the walls and doors of the temple in Jerusalem. But then Sennacherib decided to invade anyway. He sent a group of representatives to announce the coming assault so that all the people could hear and tremble. He also presented his cruel threats in writing, making sure the letter made it into the hands of the king. Sennacherib and his army of 185,000 men fully expected Hezekiah to open the gates and let them walk right in.

Here, then, is where this biblical story circles back to what we've been talking about. One of the options available to Hezekiah was escape. They could run for their lives. Take the nearest exit that led away from this impossible situation. Put distance between themselves and the problem at hand. Gather up what they could save and go into hiding.

But without telling another person or rushing to protect himself, "Hezekiah received the letter from the messengers and read it. Then he went up to the temple of the LORD and spread it out before the LORD" (19:14).

He didn't run from the pain; he turned *into* the pain. He didn't search for a way to somehow stay on the fringes of it; he sat down with the Lord, right in the middle of it.

He prayed for a miracle, expressing exactly how he felt about the situation, including the fact that the pagan tyrant Sennacherib had "ridicule[d] the living God" (verse 16). But at the close of his prayer, Hezekiah swallowed hard and humbly said, "Now, LORD our God, deliver us from his hand, so that all the kingdoms of the earth may know that you alone, LORD, are God" (verse 19).

And the Lord heard him. He even chose to wipe out the dreaded Assyrians without Hezekiah and his countrymen so much as lifting a finger (see verses 35–36). But rescue from certain disaster became possible only when a godly man dealt honestly with his desperate situation instead of trying to avoid thinking about what was happening.

Let It All Out

King David had done the same thing generations earlier. In the book of Psalms, where so many of his writings are available to us, we often see him accepting the reality of his pain and speaking boldly to the Lord in prayer about it. Psalm 32 is one of many places where he spoke about sins weighing on his heart and mind. I think all of us can relate to experiences like that, when shame and regret have felt so heavy that we didn't believe we could withstand what they were costing us, what they were doing to us. We just want to shove them away and think about something else. Surely it's not as bad as we're making it out to be, yet . . . *Ow! This hurts.* It hurts so much to think of what we've done, what we should have done, why we didn't do something else, what in the world we were thinking! You know the spiral. We all do.

In verses 3–4 David admitted he'd taken the defensive pose before, numbing himself with sleep, maybe, or distracting himself with the business of governing. He'd intentionally kept silent in an effort to avoid the brunt of his shame.

But finally he turned straight toward it and looked the pain squarely in the eye. He quit swimming toward other streams of thought that were less upsetting. Instead,

> I acknowledged my sin to you
>> and did not cover up my iniquity.
> I said, "I will confess
>> my transgressions to the LORD." (verse 5)

And then something beautiful happened:

> You forgave
>> the guilt of my sin. (verse 5)

The rest of David's psalm is a praise-filled tribute of worship to the God who met him not when he was trying to cover up his pain but when he finally became real about it—real about what was causing his sighing, what was stealing his strength in the middle of the day.

PRAY TODAY

We hope you hear what we're saying as you deal with the pain that's weighing on you today. When we talk about turning to face the hurt, we don't mean to imply you should *want* to weep, moan, and feel raw emotion as the claws of grief and sadness scrape across your heart. There's nothing holy in *wanting* to feel pain. But numbing it brings only false relief. Running from it won't result in security. Distracting yourself from it only postpones it. The pain will always find you eventually, even if you keep attempting to dodge it.

But when we surrender our human defenses to accept the pain we're feeling and "spread it out before the LORD"—all of it!—we take the first step toward healing. The hurt will not instantly disappear. And it may not all make sense. But when we get honest with God about our pain, He takes our awareness of it and heals our broken places to make us more like Him.

In order to have any chance at this kind of freedom, you'll need to make a radical commitment to a one-day mindset. Resolutely refuse to end this day without bringing all of today's hurt to His feet, no matter how bad it feels.

> Therefore let everyone who is faithful pray to you immediately.
> When great floodwaters come,
> they will not reach him.
> You are my hiding place;
> you protect me from trouble.
> You surround me with joyful shouts of deliverance. (Psalm
> 32:6–7, CSB)

Deliverance?

Yes, deliverance. For *you*.

Josh and Kelli have taught us so much as they've followed David's example. It's been humbling to watch. Although they are only in their twenties, they are walking through this incredibly heavy period in their lives. Their authenticity is inspiring. They've exhibited tremendous grace. But not by always making sure they paste a smiling face on their grief and pain. It's been bone-deep hard, but they've not sunk under it because they haven't run from it. In facing their anguish head-on, they've seen God keep doing what God always does. He's provided them a hiding place. Protected them. Delivered them.

You don't have to pray. You can rush into your day, this one day you know God has given you as a sacred gift, without talking to your Creator who loves you. It's your choice. You don't have to pray if you don't want God's direction, power, and wisdom to see the unseen. You see, you don't *have* to pray, but you *get* to pray! You can choose to experience God's presence and comfort and direction in your life this very day. Or not. The choice is yours.

Living the Lesson

You Don't Have to Pray. You Get to Pray.

What benefits of daily prayer and Bible reading were described in this chapter?

Do you sometimes feel as if reading the Bible and praying are things you *ought* to do instead of things you *get* to do? How did this chapter change your perspective?

What problems in your life have motivated you to pray more? What was the result?

As you reflect on the examples set by Hezekiah and David, what strikes you about how they dealt with their pain? In what situation do you need to lay your pain before the Lord instead of avoiding it? If you need to, write a letter to God revealing your hurt and asking Him for healing.

Have you allowed your pain to push you toward God or away from God? Today, let the pain in your life drive you to the only One who can bring healing.

It's So Hard Because the Stakes Are So High

Don't be afraid of them, because the LORD your God will fight for you.

—DEUTERONOMY 3:22, NCV

Aim at Heaven and you will get earth "thrown in": aim at earth and you will get neither.

—C. S. LEWIS

God never wastes a tear. He brings beauty from ashes and uses our pain to bring healing to others who are hurting. Even though we knew that going in, we're constantly surprised by how true it is.

But what we never really thought about until we began our journey through the valley of grief is that the Enemy tries never to waste a tear either. The Adversary is determined to wring every possible ounce of collateral damage from our pain. He will attack from every possible angle in seemingly unrelated ways as he tries to isolate us in our grief. He attempts to scratch away our hope and steal even the good memories. In the vortex of our pain, he tries to muddle our relationships with misunderstandings so that we turn on people closest to us.

God uses our tears to water seeds of life and hope, while Satan tries to use our tears to drown us. We have a God who came to give us life to the full, and an Enemy who wants to steal, kill, and destroy (see John 10:10).

Fortunately, Satan is fighting a losing battle.

The final outcome was settled when Christ defeated death and rose from the grave. He defeated everything hell could throw at Him to make a way to heaven for us.

Even though the war is won, we can lose our way. We can lose our hope, our joy, and our community—we can lose a battle—if we don't choose to live in that victory today.

This finally became clear to us in one of the most difficult, deepest valleys in our journey through grief. We were giving in to our doubts and retreating into our hurt instead of reaching out for help. Then God whispered, *Don't you see? It's so hard because the stakes are so high.*

TEARS IN A BOTTLE

The weeks leading up to Jude's diagnosis had been incredibly stressful already. Kelli was preparing for her pharmacy board exams, which of course included a lot of extra studying, reading, and reviewing, while at the same time dealing with the fatigue and other unpleasantness of pregnancy. There were many days and late nights when Josh and Kelli wished these stressful times would just hurry up and pass so they could get back to the good life.

Then, frighteningly, everything changed. For the worse. There they sat in Cincinnati, the day after their arrival, with enormous new battles to wage. Almost overnight, the annoyance of trying to find a comfortable sitting position while studying medical textbooks didn't seem nearly so unbearable. The day after we arrived, Josh said, "Wow. What we wouldn't give to have last week's troubles back."

Maybe you can relate. We're always trying to get ourselves back to a time that was easier or to move ourselves forward to a less chaotic or less complicated phase of life.

But as long as we're on this earth, part of our assignment involves reconciling what we thought we would have with what we do have.

We'd all probably agree with the general principle that hard things help us. In theory, we agree with Nietzsche's observation that "what does not kill us makes us *stronger*,"[13] but we're still surprised when trouble comes.

Our world is broken, and every person in it has a bent toward sin. So why are we always taken by surprise when life is hard? The real surprise is not that we have troubles but that we have a God who cares about them. A Creator who is distressed by our disasters. In Psalm 56:8 David said,

> You keep track of all my sorrows.
> > You have collected all my tears in your bottle.
> > You have recorded each one in your book. (NLT)

And *that* should amaze us. *That's* what should go against our expectations.

God understands something about our suffering that we don't. And He has made us a promise. Soon enough He's going to restore "the years the locusts have eaten" (Joel 2:25). Soon enough He will bestow on us

> a crown of beauty
> > instead of ashes,
> the oil of joy
> > instead of mourning,

and a garment of praise

    instead of a spirit of despair. (Isaiah 61:3)

Our wise, loving Father is totally confident in His ability to take care of us, totally confident that not one of our tears will be wasted.

For us, after Jude went to be with the Lord, it seemed as though suddenly every restaurant, every commercial, and every sidewalk was filled with parents and their new babies. The diaper ads. The strollers. The baby shower invitations. Were they always there? Maybe. But it took the attack of the Enemy to bring them circling around us as if on an endless loop.

And good for them, right? It's not as if we didn't want to be genuinely happy for people who were experiencing life with their healthy, squirmy, chubby-cheeked kids and grandkids. But when you're longing to hold your child or grandchild, whom you *could* be holding if not for a hard thing God could have prevented, it's difficult to celebrate with others.

Satan can be counted on to make the most of that scenario every day of the week. He'll take a song, a smell, a flavor of ice cream—anything he can get his hands on—and catapult you into a memory of regret or a pit of unresolved pain, whispering, *Where is your cruel, distant God now?*

Even holidays, once the best of times, can now become the worst—reminders of what you don't have, times for the Enemy to highlight your loss. We remember the sag in our hearts when Kelli should have been celebrating her first Mother's Day with baby Jude in her arms and again the next month when Josh would've been celebrating his first Father's Day. We made a point of telling this young couple who fought so valiantly for their son that they were good parents—and that they deserved to be honored with all parents whose children were looking up to them with such love and admiration on those special days.

Don't misunderstand us. We're glad there are special days set aside to honor moms and dads. Being a parent is the hardest, best, and least recognized job on the planet. But our journey with Jude has taught us something. Never again will we celebrate Mother's Day and Father's Day—or any holiday, for that matter—without saying a special prayer for all those who are aching on that day. The parents whose child is in heaven. The couple struggling with infertility. Anyone touched by any of a hundred different scenarios ending with the same crushing heartache. We've learned firsthand that this is a silent community. They're truly happy for all the kids and parents celebrating that day, but that does nothing to ease their hurt.

So what are we supposed to do? Well, here is one practical step you can take.

Say their names.

If you know grieving parents, bring up their child's name. Let them talk, and really listen. Don't say "I understand." Because unless you *personally* have had the *exact* same experience, you can't possibly understand. And that's okay. You're not expected to! It might seem like a good idea to bring up your own experiences with pain in an effort to relate. But please don't even try.

Before Jude, we would have been hesitant to mention the name of a child who had died to the parents because, in that moment, they seemed okay. We didn't want to remind them of a painful experience.

We were wrong.

Josh and Kelli helped us understand that parents who have lost a child long to hear his name. You don't have to worry about reminding them of their lost child, because they've never forgotten.

Even knowing this, we still feel awkward and inadequate when we talk to parents who have lost a child. What if we say the wrong thing? It feels safer to stay far away from the subject and stick to the weather. Believe us, we get it.

But here's the truth: we awkwardly reach out to the grieving, or we don't reach out at all. There are no other options. And we've found grieving parents to be incredibly gracious. If we gently bring it up and speak their child's name and then listen, we've yet to meet parents who weren't grateful. They may only be able to give a half smile or murmur a quick thank-you, but they walk away feeling a little less alone knowing they weren't the only ones thinking of their child that day. All parents deserve to know that their child will never be forgotten.

Chris's Story: Our Father Fights for Us

Let's think for a minute. Why would Satan need to exert this much effort to hurt us, to make us blame God, and to maximize every decibel of distress in our hearts? What's his motivation?

Could it be because the Enemy knows just how close our relationship with God can become during hard life experiences? Could it be because the testimony of our faithfulness in suffering is so damaging to the message he's trying to communicate to the world? Could it be because the stakes of life and eternity are infinitely greater than we can possibly realize?

The great news in this high-stakes, one-day-at-a-time battle is that you have a heavenly Father who fights for you. All you have to do is stand firm and trust Him.

Before Kelli came out of surgery to remove her amnioport, it was only Josh and me weathering the wait. Any minute, we thought, someone would come bursting out to tell us they were taking Jude to an ambulance in order to transfer him back to the children's hospital, where they could continue working to stabilize him and where they could swoop in with emergency measures if needed. It was only a few minutes' ride from here to there, and we'd be right behind them. *Please, God, bring somebody through that door with a face we recognize, somebody with a comforting look, somebody who'll tell us it's time for us to go. Let's get going.*

But the NICU doctor who finally came out looking for us was not one we'd previously worked with. We'd actually met her just that morning. And she didn't seem to be moving at quite the rushed pace we expected. "Can you come with me?" she asked. "I need to speak with you." We followed her into a small private consultation room. She shut the door and turned around, clearly hurting and searching for words. Other doctors were already sitting at the table.

"I'm sorry," she began. "We've decided not to transfer Jude. I'm so sorry."

What? You mean—already? Without even trying to . . . But . . . wait . . .

"You need to go and hold him now."

So this was it? They weren't even going to transfer him? At all? The finality clutched at my throat. We'd waited so long for another outcome. And now . . . we had to say goodbye?

But what could we say? They'd made up their minds. It just hadn't worked. The process hadn't worked. We could sit here asking more questions, of course—and we did!—but clearly we weren't going to be able to do anything to alter their decision.

Until Josh said, "Doctor, I'm *asking* you to transfer him."

With compassion and poise, the doctor reiterated her reasoned conclusions, which included some of the same benchmark numbers and terminology we'd been learning by heart, the various metrics of viability.

She obviously knew what she was talking about and was firm about what needed to take place, despite how she regretted saying it.

But Josh was firm as well—not in a belligerent, won't-take-no-for-an-answer manner or with a refusal to understand. He just wasn't about to let the first word from the first doctor, giving us the first postpartum report on his first child's condition, be the last word.

Jude was still alive. Even if only barely. And Josh was not going to stop pushing until *everything* possible had been done to save his son's life.

Over the next few hours, he spoke with some of the other doctors we'd encountered throughout this process, including heads of departments. All the voices I could overhear sounded professional, composed, and courteous, explaining with frank thoroughness why they agreed with what their colleague had said, along with their deepest, sincerest sympathies. Nothing, they each repeated, was pointing to Jude's survival.

"I understand that, Doctor; I do," Josh finally said, realizing he'd ascended to the top of the chain of command. "Honestly, I do hear what you're saying. But I'm saying *this*. This is my son. And all I'm asking is that you look at him. All I'm asking is that you try. I know the odds are infinitesimally low. We knew it from the moment we came here. We know it now more than ever. But as long as he's breathing, as long as he's still alive"—my son's forceful voice now broke into a whisper—"I'm just asking you not to close the door. Don't give up. Please."

And to their credit, they didn't. By the next morning all the doctors he'd spoken with, instead of merely accepting what they'd seen on the write-ups, came to examine Jude for themselves.

But the thing that stood out the most to me in that bold interchange between Josh and the various medical staff was not the presence of multiple doctors who strode into the intensive care unit to look at Jude nor the sad, somber agreement that each one shared with us concerning his condition. What I saw most clearly was a father fighting passionately for his child. As long as Jude had breath, his daddy would fight for him. It represented for me an unseen reality that happens every day in my behalf and yours.

The Bible says of Jesus, "He entered heaven itself, now to appear for us in God's presence" (Hebrews 9:24). Having been raised from the dead, "Christ Jesus . . . is at the right hand of God and is also interceding for us" (Romans 8:34). Indeed, He "*always* lives to intercede" for us (Hebrews 7:25, emphasis added). Jesus, knowing every need in our hearts, is continually serving as our representative before the Father, advocating for us by the force of His own name and His relationship with us.

Are you feeling more discouraged today than you feel on most days? Are you carrying burdens too heavy for you, whether for yourself or for someone else? Do you consider yourself a lost cause, thinking God has probably given you all the help and second chances you're likely to get? Know this: Somewhere today in a place beyond your seeing, Jesus is going to bat for you. He is motioning toward the throne with scarred hands, from which His blood flowed out for your sins, and He is declaring that He will *not* give up on you.

Living the Lesson

It's So Hard Because the Stakes Are So High

Describe a time when you fell into regret or unresolved pain and were tempted to doubt God's goodness. What was the outcome? How can you combat similar situations in the future?

Write down the name of someone you know who is grieving the loss of a loved one. How can you pray specifically for her? Seize the next opportunity to speak to her and mention her loved one, and then listen with a compassionate heart.

Read 2 Chronicles 20:17. Have you been trying to fight a battle without God's strength? In what battle do you need to stand firm and watch God fight for you?

Read Matthew 11:28–30. Let the words of Jesus speak directly to your situation. What heavy burdens are you carrying today that you need to lay at Jesus's feet?

Write a prayer to your heavenly Father thanking Him for His fierce love and strong protection.

There Is a Hidden Gift in Every Hurt

At first I didn't think of it as a gift, and begged God to remove it. Three times I did that, and then he told me,

> My grace is enough; it's all you need.
> My strength comes into its own in your weakness.

—2 CORINTHIANS 12:8–9, MSG

We are not human beings on a spiritual journey. We are spiritual beings on a human journey.

—ATTRIBUTED TO PIERRE TEILHARD DE CHARDIN

N ot long ago we were up in the Northeast, a section of the country where we hadn't spent a lot of time before. We'd always wanted to visit the national park in Gettysburg, Pennsylvania, site of the famous Civil War battle and, of course, the Gettysburg Address delivered by Abraham Lincoln.

In November 1863, following the battle in July that had claimed the lives of thousands of soldiers, President Lincoln arrived in Gettysburg from Washington. He'd been invited to participate in a service at a cemetery near the battleground where the dead had been brought for burial. You probably remember hearing in school how the featured speaker of the day, Edward Everett, rambled on for more than two yawning hours, saying nothing that anyone remembers.[14]

Then President Lincoln took the stage, and in fewer than three hundred words, he captured the spirit of the moment in such concise eloquence that we've never forgotten it.

The reason we take you along for a moment on our little trip to Pennsylvania is because of something that struck us as we walked around the fields where that bloody battle was fought. They'd come there, Lincoln said, to "dedicate a portion of that field, as a final resting place" for those who'd died fighting for a united nation.

But that's not all Lincoln said. This is the part that spoke to us:

> In a larger sense, we can not dedicate—we can not consecrate—we can not hallow—this ground. The brave men, living and dead, who struggled here, have consecrated it, far above our poor power to add or detract. . . . It is for us the living, rather, to be dedicated here to the unfinished work which they who fought here have thus far so nobly advanced. It is rather for us to be here dedicated to the great task remaining before us.[15]

A staggering 51,000 young men had died at Gettysburg.[16] Most, if not all, of Lincoln's audience that day had lost a son, husband, brother, or father. They were aching with loss.

The crowd had come to the ceremony to honor the battlefield, but before they left, they'd been charged with carrying on the fight.

In other words, let your pain change you.

If you're hurting today, you don't need to figure out to whom or to what it is dedicated. Just be open to letting the pain change you. Allow it to help make you into a different, more compassionate person. The stuff we go through in life, the heartache that characterizes so much of what we experience in this broken world, dedicates us.

Today's pain is hard, but it can do something important *inside us*.

God can employ our pain to set us apart for a greater use, for more of His sacred purposes. The sharpness of our pain and loss enables us to commit ourselves to a more devoted way of life. The thing that feels like it just might kill us can be part of how God keeps us alive, how He makes us more fully prepared for the "great task remaining before us."

Jude taught us that the main thing isn't what's happening to us but what's happening through us.

CHRIS'S STORY: HIDDEN GIFTS

There is a gift hidden within every deep pain. Did you hear that? It is the gift of being able to empathize. It is the gift of being able to say everything without saying anything at all. It is the gift of being able to display biblical truth in living color so that hope and joy spring up inside caverns of despair.

Humans are born with the ability to hear sounds only within a limited range of frequency. However, various animals can hear different frequencies. Dogs, for instance, react to certain whistles that produce pitches beyond what we can detect. In the same way, pain has a unique capability of broadening the range of what you can "hear" emotionally and spiritually. It increases your ability to pinpoint the places where others are hurting and know what they need—sometimes even more than they do.

Jude's death was not a good situation. Obviously.

Neither was my mom's death when I was a teenager. She died from cancer at an early age, and I faced the prospect of graduation and college, and of marriage and motherhood one day, without the counsel and camaraderie of my mom.

It wasn't something I talked about a lot. I remember several months after her death trying to cope with it by training in hospice care. I thought

I could help others walk through their own battles with cancer. After attending all the classes, I was told I was the youngest certified hospice caregiver in the state. I couldn't wait to be assigned a patient! I was going to help the person's family *so much*! As it turned out, all my encouraging words were swallowed in tears. It just hurt too much. I hadn't allowed myself to deal with what had happened to my own family, and I ended up being devastated all over again. The pain was just staggering. I think I sort of walled it off after that.

But as Josh and I stood in that hotel hallway on the day Jude died, sobbing together, he asked me something he'd never asked before. "How did you do it, Mom? How did you make it after your mom died?"

When I heard his question, it was almost as if a flash went off. *Could my experience help my son at a time like this?* I'd never lost a child. I'd never been pregnant and not enjoyed the delight of coming home with a rosy-faced, healthy baby. But I did know how it felt when a person I thought my whole world depended on was suddenly gone, when my worst-case scenario happened. How did I keep going *then*? What did I do next?

I was fully aware that no words on this earth could soothe the places in Josh's heart that were utterly inconsolable. But—

Read this slowly because it might sound callous at first, but I think you'll know what I mean if you let it marinate. I was actually grateful in that moment, not that my mom had died but that her death gave me a connection to my son. I was able to be there for him in a way I couldn't have been otherwise. My experience with loss validated my words and helped him know he would come out on the other side of this devastating loss one day, even though he felt sure then that he never would.

If someone had told me at my mom's funeral that something good could come from her death, I'd never have trusted another word of counsel from that person. I didn't know—couldn't even have dreamed—that someday I'd be a mom myself and that I would be able to minister to my son because of my own loss. The loss of someone so dear to my heart that I could comfort him during those first maddening hours.

More than thirty years after my mom died, the gift from my pain was finally revealed. And it was worth the wait.

A FLOOD OF HEALING

After Hurricane Harvey struck Texas in 2017, causing record flooding and widespread devastation throughout the Houston area, we felt totally overwhelmed with all the needs in our church family and city.

Shortly after the rain stopped and while the floodwaters were still rising, our friends and mentors Pastor Rick and Kay Warren and Pastor Tom and Chaundel Holladay called to let us know they were on their way to Houston. They were coming to encourage us and other pastors in the area since we were on the front lines of bringing relief in the middle of the disaster.

They came at just the right time, when we needed encouragement as we cared for people who'd lost everything. Rick shared with us something very personal and profound that he and Kay were learning as they walked through the agony of grieving the death of their son Matthew. He said, "When you experience loss, it's important to remember—you'll never get over it, but you will get through it!" Then he added, "And you'll also be there to help others get through it."

His words held enormous weight for every person in the room, not because he pastored a large church but because he had endured unimaginable pain. Instead of hiding away in their own intense grief, Rick and Kay were choosing to do whatever they could to help other people make it through hard times. They refused to let pain be their isolator. Instead, it was their motivator.

Tom and Chaundel had been motivated to come to our waterlogged city by pain of a different kind. Thirty years earlier, when their kids were little, Tom and Chaundel lived in Northern California and lost everything they owned to a flood. They were only a half hour from their house when word came that the water was rising rapidly, growing dangerously high in their neighborhood. Still, by the time they got home, the damage was done.

So they understood from personal experience what it's like to see your home destroyed by flood. They knew how it feels to go through that door for the first time, into the place where you've done so much living and sharing and eating and laughing, and see everything reduced to soggy decay. They knew the pit-of-your-stomach emptiness of realizing that you now own nothing—that both the replaceable and the irreplaceable are gone. They knew exactly what it's like to stare ahead into countless days of phone calls and unbudgeted expenses and searching for temporary shelter for yourself and your children.

Tom and Chaundel had felt it all, so they came to Houston to lend a hand and offer a shoulder to cry on, to tell a shell-shocked community of sufferers that God cares and that losses heal.

But these losses you don't forget. And because this was happening at the same time our own family was healing from Jude's recent passing, we were probably a little more open to the lesson God needed to teach us.

We don't pretend to know all the ways He works. We don't know why our city was brought to a deadly standstill. We don't know why we were given the opportunity to offer our church as a refuge to desperate people, providing warm bedding and hot meals and a sturdy roof over their heads. And we don't know why, three decades earlier, our dear friends and their family went through a similar experience. God doesn't tell us these things. But we do know that out of Tom and Chaundel's private pain came direct relief to us and many others. Their firsthand experience with a specific type of loss enabled them to speak to and love people in situations that not everyone could relate to as readily.

We could see it clearly: their pain was others' gain.

Is it possible that God, in His superintending sovereignty over everything that exists, allowed something hard in Tom and Chaundel's life thirty years before to show them how to depend on Him more completely? Was that His sole intent—communicating through a painful weather-related experience something that would be important to their faith throughout their lives? Or did part of His plan for allowing a flood to touch their family so severely on the West Coast in the 1980s include bringing blessing to people in Texas decades later?

And, if so, should we be willing to trust a God who would allow our hurt to help others?

WINS FROM LOSSES

Romans 8:28 is often cherry-picked out of context to mean something it doesn't exactly say.

> We know that in all things God works for the good of those who love him, who have been called according to his purpose.

Our eyes latch on to that first part about how God can turn "all things" into something "good"—a message we love hearing and believing without always recognizing that this promise is based on our relationship with Him and on His larger mission for our lives. This verse doesn't say that everything that happens is good; rather, it says that He is able to bring about good from even the worst situations.

That means if we experience something that seems entirely bad, it's because we don't yet see it as the good thing God will one day make of it, even if that doesn't happen until He makes all things right in heaven.

If we look to the example of Christ, we realize this "good" may not be just for ourselves. The bad things that happen to us can result in good things for other people too. As Paul said—again, right here in Romans 8—"He who did not spare his own Son, but gave him up *for us all*—how will he not also, along with him, graciously give us all things?" (verse 32, emphasis added).

Does God want good things for us? Jesus is the only answer to that question we should ever need.

Jesus was tortured, beaten, humiliated—killed—not for His own benefit but for ours. Good Friday, after all, was good for us, not for Jesus!

We always want to be extremely careful not to misinterpret the Scriptures. It is so easy to read something into them that's not there. But looking at what Jesus has done for us, we see how it's not beyond the power and mercy of God to transform our pain—whatever we're going through—so that in His abundant love He can use it to spread good all over the place. Maybe our suffering, like Jesus's suffering, is sometimes allowed in order to benefit someone else.

All we know is that since Jude went to be with the Lord, the people who've also dealt with the loss of a child or grandchild are the ones who've been able to minister to us most. When those people heard about what happened, they instantly reached out. And the help and healing—the goodness—that have flowed to us as a result have been on a different level of compassion. The pain of their past has been instrumental in mending the pain of our present.

Many people who haven't been through this same trial have expressed care for us, and we thank God for every one of them. They are precious to us, and we've needed all of them desperately for help and support. But the ones who understand our pain because they've been there have given us hope.

The fact that they're still standing. Thriving even! That gives us courage.

And we believe this is part of what God intends to take place in the body of Christ. No one who's hurting is meant to suffer alone.

Your struggle, as intense as it may be, is part of something bigger.

God Never Wastes a Hurt

At the Ronald McDonald House in Cincinnati—which was an absolute blessing to our family—we met the parents of a little boy named Judah, who had the same condition as Jude. Judah, though, had been born before we arrived and was still in the NICU on dialysis. That was our dream for Jude—to make it to dialysis. It's what all of us were praying for. And if that meant we needed to stay there for a year in order for Jude to develop and grow, we were more than willing to do so. Judah's family was a real encouragement. A living success story of the procedure's possibilities.

Judah's parents were actually from Houston as well, and during our stay in Cincinnati, the doctors determined that Judah was well enough to be transferred home to Texas Children's Hospital. He was about four months old.

Then February came. Josh and Kelli were back home by this time too, grieving hard, when they received a call from Judah's mom and dad, saying their little baby boy had taken a turn for the worse. We rushed downtown to see them and sat with them through that long day, just praying and listening. Soon it became apparent that Judah wasn't going to rally, and despite having been one of the few who'd broken through and made it, he died shortly thereafter.

This was so hard. One of those situations when you're just not sure you can keep on living. But we watched with awe as Josh and Kelli dug in deep and served these other young parents as we had done for them only a short time before. They helped plan the funeral, talked them through the process of locating a burial plot, and walked them through a hundred details that no young parents should ever have to know.

There was *so much pain* that went along with that. Josh and Kelli couldn't help feeling it, like a scab being ripped open and made to bleed again. But they took it on just as Christ took on pain for us. They accepted the fact that God had chosen for them to go forward in life without being able to hold their son, Jude, in their arms. But they would do good with what was left—with the "gift" of pain He *had* trusted them to steward.

Their arms ached for Jude—almost more now, as they lived through another family's loss that so closely paralleled their own. But their pain became another's gain.

And that's not all bad, is it?

It just takes a change of heart to see this truth and live it out. It takes learning how to humbly receive comfort at others' expense, as well as devote ourselves to caring for others at our own expense.

This is how the body of Christ works. We lean on one another for stability and take on one another's pain for safekeeping. It's not always an easy road to walk or an easy teaching to follow. But if life is going to be hard anyway, why not make it worth it? Why not determine to wring every ounce of good out of every bad situation? Why not see whether

God might take the most awful events of your life and convert them into a blessing that reverberates into eternity?

KERRY'S STORY: DON'T HIDE YOUR SCARS

After Jesus rose from the dead, He appeared to His disciples, but Thomas wasn't there. The disciples, of course, let Thomas know that he'd missed the big event and that Jesus was truly alive!

We call him doubting Thomas, but really he was just human Thomas. I think every one of us would have had similar doubts and felt the same confusion. Just a few days before, Thomas had seen his Messiah cruelly nailed to a cross. He had seen Him buried in a tomb carved in the rock and a huge stone rolled over the entrance. As far as Thomas could see, it was over! All hope had died with Jesus on the cross.

Thomas said he wouldn't believe until he could touch Jesus's nail-scarred hands and the wound in His side. Well, the next week Thomas got that chance as Jesus appeared again and said to Thomas, "Put your finger here; see my hands. Reach out your hand and put it into my side. Stop doubting and believe" (John 20:27).

Of course, Thomas did believe!

Have you ever stopped to think about the fact that Jesus still had the scars in His hands and side from the Crucifixion even after He rose from the dead? Christ has a resurrected body, but He chose to keep the scars. Why?

His scars told the story! His scars reminded Thomas and every one of us that He took the nails so we could be forgiven and free.

Jesus's scars tell the story that I no longer have to carry around guilt and shame for all my mess-ups. His scars shout to me that my sins are paid for.

Every scar tells a story. I have a scar on my right knee that I've had since I was six years old. I had just learned to ride a bike, and on my high-handlebar, banana-seat Schwinn bicycle, I thought I was the real deal.

One afternoon our family was going on a bike ride, and as we approached a steep hill, my mom cautioned me to keep my brakes on the whole way down so I wouldn't get going too fast and lose control. Well, I thought that advice didn't apply to a bike-riding genius like me, so sure enough I got going so fast that I lost control of the bike and crashed into the gravel on the side of the road. After the tears and blood were all wiped away, I was taken to the doctor's office, where he used a scalpel to cut out a pebble embedded in my knee. He gave me the small rock, I guess as sort of a warning to remember to listen to my parents next time. I lost the rock long ago, but I still have the scar that tells the story of my obstinate stupidity!

Every scar tells a story. Our scars don't tell the story of our hurts—they tell the story of our Healer. Our scars point us to the One with the nail scars in His hands and feet. Jesus kept His scars to show you and me how much He loves us and how valuable we are to Him.

The church should be a community of people who no longer have to hide their scars.

The teenager who looks down at the scars on his arms from cutting and is filled with shame needs to know that the One who bears the scars on His body because He took all our shame on the cross says he is treasured and loved.

The woman who believes the lie that she is beautiful only if she is stick thin and looks like a supermodel needs to look to the One with the scars on His body. He'll show her the truth: She is worth dying for. She is beautiful and valuable and more than enough.

The men and women running on the treadmill of success, trying to prove they've got what it takes, need to look to the One with the scars on His hands and side. He says they can stop trying to prove their worth, because that was settled on the cross. They can rest in His love.

The ones who are stuck in the vicious cycle of addiction and feel as if there's no hope need to know they can look to our nail-scarred Savior, who died for them and set them free.

If you are broken and wounded, our nail-scarred Savior asks you to bring your brokenness to Him, the only one who can heal. He pleads with you to never hide your scars, because your scars tell the story—not of your hurt but of His healing power. Your scars tell the story of God's glory.

> I am convinced that neither death nor life, neither angels nor demons, neither the present nor the future, nor any powers, neither height nor depth, nor anything else in all creation, will be able to separate us from the love of God that is in Christ Jesus our Lord. (Romans 8:38–39)

There is no pain God can't use for His greater purposes. Would you let Him use yours?

Living the Lesson

There Is a Hidden Gift in Every Hurt

It's hard to see the gifts hidden in our problems unless we take time to look for them. Name a challenge you're currently facing, and think of a possible gift that might be hidden in it.

How has your loss or pain changed you? In what ways has it made you more sensitive to the pain of others?

Read Romans 8:28. How has God used your suffering to bring about good for someone else?

We often hide our struggles because we're afraid of rejection, but the truth is that revealing our scars draws us closer to others and points them to our Healer. Have you ever experienced a time when acknowledging your struggles encouraged someone else? Briefly describe it.

Are you ready to allow God to turn your hurt into a source of healing for others? What's one step you could take to make that happen?

The Number of Your Days Is Unrelated to the Impact of Your Life

Do not forget this one thing, dear friends: With the Lord a day is like a thousand years, and a thousand years are like a day.

—2 Peter 3:8

Some people arrive and make such a beautiful impact on your life, you can barely remember what life was like without them.

—Anna Taylor

That first Christmas after Jude died really hurt. The Christmas before, we'd been camped out in a room down the street from the children's hospital, more than a thousand miles from our own family room, fireplace, and Christmas tree. Although we were back home again, where we'd celebrated so many Christmases past, we were there without the grandson we'd anticipated being part of it for his first time.

We included a stocking for him, of course, tacked up on the mantelpiece with the ones for our other grandchildren. Ben, Joanna, Jude. All three precious names in a row. It felt so right to have his stocking hanging there—Jude was a part of our family whether he was with us or in heaven.

But while our other grandchildren's stockings were filled with candy and toys and other fun things for them to open and enjoy, Jude's stocking was being filled with something else.

As December neared, we'd decided to go looking for someone who needed some extra love that Christmas, the way we'd needed it in Cincinnati the year before. We wanted to remind someone who needed to hear it that love was on the way. We found a family in our church whose husband had recently been deployed, leaving his wife and two young boys—a baby and a toddler—to spend Christmas without him.

We couldn't relate exactly, of course, but from the viewpoint of our own crisis, we knew how life can rudely interfere with people's plans, changing the way they'd hoped to spend Christmas with their family.

Many kind friends and extended family members wanted to share Jude's message of love too, so they contributed to an unofficial fund in Jude's Christmas stocking. We turned those checks and cash into a care package that we mailed to the dad in this family at his overseas location, as well as a few extra gifts for the two little boys and their mom, who were alone on Christmas Day.

We didn't do anything special, really. Nothing heroic or sacrificial, nothing more than what a lot of people do to brighten others' spirits during the holidays. But for us it was the Christmas version of our everyday, all-the-time commitment that arose from the one-day difference Jude had made in our lives.

We told you from the start that Jude's life didn't go the way we'd have chosen. But his story has. In our Miracle Book we recorded the prayer dearest to our hearts: "Jesus Christ, may Jude Samuel contend for the faith and reflect Your glory to his generation."

And he is.

That's because in the end, the number of our days on earth is wholly unrelated to the size of our spirits or the impact of our lives. Despite the short time he was here, Jude is a heavyweight in heaven.

We're constantly reminded of that by people who tell us that Jude has changed them. They tell us their compassion for Jude has led them to uncommon ground. Here's one example of hundreds of stories we've been told:

Josh and Kelli,

I know today, January 7, is Jude's second birthday. Happy birthday, Jude.

I want to share a story about how Jude has influenced me and others.

Josh, your mother had called me and told me about Jude's prognosis not long after you found out. My husband and I started praying for Jude. He asked me what we could do that was tangible for you. I told him we couldn't really do anything tangible because you were leaving for Cincinnati that day. He still prayed for that anyway.

Later that day I was in the grocery store. I got in the shortest line. After I put everything from my basket onto the counter to check out, I realized the couple in front of me was having difficulty. Their credit card wasn't going through. The cashier had them try several times. I didn't roll my eyes or sigh with frustration because of the holdup, but I prayed with every try that their card would go through. During this process I noticed that the woman was pregnant and that they had a toddler in the child seat of the cart. I also noticed that their bill was over $200. I kept praying that their card would work.

Eventually, they pushed their cart to the side and started to leave. But just then Jesus clearly told me to pay their bill. I stepped up to the cashier and said I would pay. The woman hugged me and began to cry. The man hugged me and thanked me. I told them Jesus loves them and wanted me to help. Then the cashier and all the other cashiers hugged me and started crying. I was crying too.

I know that Jesus orchestrated this for Jude. He heard our prayer and allowed us to do something tangible for the three of you. He made that happen His way.

God bless you and your baby, Jude Samuel.

Love,

Kari

THE BLESSING CONTINUES

A year and a half after Jude went to be with the Lord, his little sister was born. Josh and Kelli named her Mary Love—Mary, in honor of Chris's mom, and Love, because she fulfilled God's promise in Jude 1:2 that "love is on the way!" (MSG).

Only someone who hasn't lost a child could imagine that giving birth to one baby would make up for the loss of another. Mary Love is an absolute joy in her own right. She isn't a replacement, nor was she ever meant to be. We have no doubt that the Lord has created a special path for this little warrior princess to forge on her own. Jude's sister will have a story all her own.

Kelli's pregnancy was rough. Still grieving deeply for Jude and fighting fear for Mary Love, Josh and Kelli leaned hard into the lessons they'd learned from Jude.

They kept their focus limited to the day they were living in. They found reasons to be grateful for even the most uncomfortable aspects of pregnancy, like nausea, because they meant things were progressing the way they should. They fought the urge to retreat and kept an eye out for people they could encourage.

Finally Mary Love arrived! Ask anyone whom she looked like, and they'll tell you: Jude.

If you're a parent, you probably remember what it's like to care for a screaming newborn who has her days and nights mixed up. There's a reason sleep deprivation is considered a torture tactic under the Geneva Conventions. Sure, you may have pulled an all-nighter at some point, but being a new parent means going for *weeks* without being able to string together more than a few hours of sleep. It makes you irritable. Grouchy. Mean even. And who could blame you?

That's probably why an offhand comment Josh made when Mary Love was a few weeks old hit us like a thunderbolt. We'd stopped by their house to help out for a couple of hours after Kelli and Josh had spent another sleepless night. Josh answered the door with his hair sticking up, in yesterday's rumpled clothes, spit-up on his shoulder. He was holding Mary Love, who was red faced and screaming with that uniquely grating, gasping cry of a newborn.

Now, Kelli is great at decorating and organizing, and their little house usually looks homey and inviting. But on this morning it looked as if a baby-supply bomb had gone off. We followed Josh into the nursery as he mumbled details like when she was due for her next bottle, Mary Love still crying nonstop. As he was talking, he started to change her diaper, and the moment he removed the wet one, she pooped.

That's when he looked up and said, "You know, Kelli and I were just talking, *and this is pretty great.*"

That statement broke our hearts in the best, hardest way. Even through the pounding headache of sleeplessness, even when he'd eaten nothing but cold cereal for days, even with vomit on his shoulder and poop on his hands, he never lost sight of the gift. What a privilege to *get* to comfort Mary Love when she cried. To hear her cries at all.

It's *all* a gift. Mary Love no more, or less, than Jude.

Even though he's not here with us, the wonder is that we got to know him at all. Nothing we'd done had merited spending a whole day with that perfect boy. The question wasn't "Why him?" but "Why us?" Not "Why didn't Jude get everything?" but "Why did we get *anything*?"

Jude Samuel Shook ran his particular race to the full. As he ran, first his parents and then others have become his megaphone to a world that desperately needs to hear his profound, simple message: *Come and know my Savior.*

Years later, people are still responding to that call.

So maybe one day was enough after all.

Living the Lesson

The Number of Your Days Is Unrelated to the Impact of Your Life

What are you doing with your one and only life that will make a difference when you're gone?

How has adopting a one-day mindset helped you live more intentionally?

What is the most important lesson you have learned from this book, and how can you continue to live this lesson on a daily basis?

Read Jude 1:1–2 one more time: "I, Jude, am a slave to Jesus Christ and brother to James, writing to those loved by God the Father, called and kept safe by Jesus Christ. Relax, everything's going to be all right; rest, everything's coming together; open your hearts, love is on the way!" (MSG). What encourages you the most about the promise that one day "everything's going to be all right"?

Write a letter to God asking Him to help you unwrap the gift of this one day and each new day He blesses you with.

Acknowledgments

Jude's story has been shaped by countless individuals who chose to honor the life of a little boy they hadn't met. We have no doubt that someday Jude will greet those people with a big hug and thank them himself. Until then, we'd like to offer our bone-deep gratitude to the following people:

- Jude's family—the Ingrams, Nelsons, Shooks, Alphas, Copelands, and Jensens.
- Friends who feel like family—the Reeves, Millers, Shermans, Montgomerys, Webbs, Smiths, Ramirezes, Quinns, Meltons, Bookers, Hymels, Lewises, Johansons, and Mathwigs.
- Woodlands Church family—you blessed us in a thousand ways.
- Dr. Elizabeth Becker, Dr. Foong-Yen Lim, Dr. Bill Polzin, and the staff of the Cincinnati Fetal Center.
- The people of Cincinnati—during our time in your city, we wrote you a letter but never knew where to send it. How do you send a letter to a whole city? Happily, we just found a way.

Dear Cincinnati,

Our little family showed up in your city at the darkest moment of our lives. A few days earlier, doctors in our hometown of Houston had given us devastating news. Suddenly we were on the doorstep of the only place that offered hope, Cincinnati Children's Hospital.

You didn't know we were coming, Cincinnati. No one had told you our story: how we'd spent the past few sleepless nights sobbing on the nursery floor; how the lack of hope had nearly stolen our ability to breathe. We were hurting so deeply that we had no tears, no words, and no emotion left to explain what was going on. So we didn't even try.

We walked among you like empty, dazed shells. We were the ones who forgot to go when the light turned green. We were the people ahead of you on the crowded sidewalk who stopped without warning, wondering which way to turn. We were the ones who held up the line as we stared blankly at the menu board. We inconvenienced you, and we didn't even seem to care.

And do you know what you did in return, Cincinnati? You were overwhelmingly, inconceivably kind to us. Every. Single. Day.

When we were exasperating, you were smiling and patient.

When we looked confused, you stopped to give directions.

When we were numb, you gave us grace.

So we just have to thank you, Cincinnati. Your culture of kindness was like oxygen to our souls. Whatever troubles you may face or differences you may have as a city, we hope you show as much patience and kindness to one another as you did to us.

We will always be your biggest fans.

Our deepest gratitude is reserved for Jesus Christ. Your plan is higher than ours.

Your eyes saw me when I was still an unborn child.
Every day of my life was recorded in your book
before one of them had taken place. (Psalm 139:16,
God's Word)

Notes

1. John K. Coyle, "How the Greeks Hacked Time: Kairos Versus Chronos," *Art of Really Living* (blog), November 25, 2018, www.theartofreallyliving.com/taorlblog/2018/11/25/ how-the -greeks-hacked-timenbspkairos-versus-chronos.

2. Coyle, "How the Greeks Hacked Time."

3. Henri J. M. Nouwen and Philip Roderick, *Beloved: Henri Nouwen in Conversation* (London: Canterbury Press Norwich, 2007), 39.

4. All Sons & Daughters, "Great Are You, Lord," by David Leonard, Jason Ingram, and Leslie Jordan, *Live,* Integrity Music, 2013.

5. "Why We Wear Black to a Funeral," *Cremation Blog,* Une Belle Vie, https://decorative-urns.com/cremation-blog/managing-grief /why-we-wear-black-to-a-funeral.

6. To read the Bible stories mentioned, see the following passages: Genesis 3–4 (Adam and Eve); Genesis 22:1–19 (Abraham and Isaac); Genesis 29; 35:16–18 (Jacob and Rachel); Genesis 37; 39–41 (Joseph); Exodus 1:22–3:10 (Moses); Numbers 14:18–23; Deuteronomy 34 (the Israelites); 1 Samuel 15:17–29 (Saul); 2 Samuel 11–12 (David); 1 Kings 4:20–34; 11:1–6 (Solomon).

7. See Ezekiel 37:1–14 for this story.

8. C. S. Lewis, *The Screwtape Letters* (New York: HarperCollins, 2001), 40.

9. Corrie ten Boom, *Jesus Is Victor* (Old Tappan, NJ: Revell, 1984), 183.

10. Josh Shook, "Restore the Years," *Live,* Woodlands Worship, 2019.

11. E. P. Sanders, *Encyclopaedia Britannica,* s.v. "St. Paul the Apostle," www.britannica.com/biography/Saint-Paul-the-Apostle.

12. See 2 Corinthians 1:8–10; 6:3–10; 7:5–7; 11:22–28.

13. Friedrich Nietzsche, *Writings from the Late Notebooks,* ed. Rüdiger Bittner, trans. Kate Sturge (Cambridge: Cambridge University Press, 2003), 188.

14. Ted Widmer, "The Other Gettysburg Address," *New York Times,* November 19, 2013, https://opinionator.blogs.nytimes.com/2013 /11/19/the-other-gettysburg-address.

15. Abraham Lincoln, The Gettysburg Address (speech, Gettysburg, PA, November 19, 1863), www.abrahamlincolnonline.org/lincoln /speeches/gettysburg.htm.

16. "Battle of Gettysburg: Facts, Summary and HistoryNet Articles About the Battle of Gettysburg During the American Civil War," HistoryNet, www.historynet.com/battle-of-gettysburg.